MEMOIRS
OF A
RECOVERING
AUTOCRAT

MEMOIRS
OF A
RECOVERING
AUTOCRAT

**Revealing Insights for Managing
the Autocrat in All of Us**

RICHARD W. HALLSTEIN

Berrett-Koehler Publishers
San Francisco

Berrett-Koehler Publishers, Inc.
155 Montgomery St.
San Francisco, CA 94104-4109
Tel: 415-288-0260   Fax: 415-362-2512

Ordering Information
Individual sales. Berrett-Koehler publications are available through most bookstores. They can
also be ordered direct from Berrett-Koehler at the address above.

Quantity sales. Special discounts are available on quantity purchases by corporations, associations, and others. For details, contact the "Special Sales Department" at the Berrett-Koehler
address above.

Orders for college textbook/course adoption use. Please contact Berrett-Koehler Publishers at
the address above.

Orders by U.S. trade bookstores and wholesalers. Please contact Publishers Group West, P.O.
Box 8843, Emeryville, CA 94662; 510-658-3453; 1-800-788-3123.

Printed in the United States of America

Printed on acid-free and recycled paper that meets the strictest state and U.S. guidelines for recycled paper (50 percent recycled waste, including 10 percent post-
consumer waste).

Library of Congress Cataloging-in-Publication Data

Hallstein, Richard W., 1940–
    Memoirs of a recovering autocrat: revealing insights for managing the autocrat
in all of us / by Richard W. Hallstein.
      p.   cm.
    Includes bibliographical references and index.
    ISBN 1-881052-35-4 (alk. paper)
    1. Decentralization in management—United States. 2. Command and control
systems–United States. 3. Hallstein, Richard W., 1940– . 4. Chief executive officers—
United States—Biography. I. Title.
HD50.H35   1993   93-8187
658.4'02—dc20   CIP

First Edition
First Printing July 1993

Cover and Book Design by Hedstrom/Blessing, Inc., Minneapolis, Minnesota

*This book is dedicated to my wife, Karen Moran,
and my adult children, Lynn, Denice, and Jon,
all of whom make constant and loving contributions
to my recovery and happiness.*

TABLE OF CONTENTS

TABLE OF CONTENTS

PREFACE

One of the readers of my first manuscript for this book strongly suggested that I change the title. His recommendation was based on the fact that he didn't identify with being an autocrat, even though he did acknowledge being autocratic at times.

Another friend who is a management consultant told me that she had many clients who would benefit from the book, but she was afraid that they would be offended by the accusation that they were autocrats.

The most alarming response came when someone told me that they couldn't wait for the book to be published, because they had many people to whom they wanted to send copies anonymously!

In spite of these objections and concerns or, perhaps, because of them, I decided to stick with the title. It is my hope that by naming and putting a spotlight on my own difficulties in overcoming autocratic behaviors, others will be more inclined to view this quite normal struggle as a small (or large) part of all of us.

A CEO and friend reported that every effective executive he ever knew was an autocrat. Further, it was his contention that being an autocrat is an essential characteristic for successful leaders.

There's no denying the need for tough-minded leaders who are capable of making difficult decisions and forcefully exerting their personal vision. To overcome the hammer's proverbial inclination to see everything as a nail, however, this book presents a powerful alternate vision of participative management that is increasingly required in our changing world.

This book is, by business standards, quite intimate. Readers accustomed to more traditional management literature might draw back from the levels of self-disclosure included in my stories. The fact is that the book might fit comfortably in any one of several areas in your favorite bookstore: management, recovery, personal growth, religion, or the men's section. I hope you will find this unusual "crossover" between living and managing intriguing, integrative, and helpful. In these pages you will find what you can't learn from Peter Drucker about living and what you won't learn from Robert Bly about managing!

Managers throughout the world are under a lot of pressure to change. At the same time that they're being asked to jettison the controlling and authoritative behaviors they've relied on for past successes, they're also being pressured to get more done with less resources. This can be a frightening and confusing proposition.

The first rule of wing walking applies: "Don't let go of the first strut until you have your hands on the next one." Many managers don't need further convincing that their old ways aren't working, but they do need a new vision of something they can grab on to that will carry them safely into the future.

On the other hand, you will find no ready formulas here. One senior executive told me he could clearly relate to the management problems and difficulties identified in the book, but he was disappointed that there weren't more concrete answers.

It's a fair criticism that some answers are missing. I've identified some intense dilemmas, polarities, and paradoxes that raise as many questions as answers. I can, however, report that to a large degree I have discovered that many of "the answers" in real life can be found by paying close attention to the questions.

Much of the current literature seems to imply that if managers were of a right spirit or mind they would abandon their old controlling ways immediately. I wish to make it clear that the rules for creating more participative cultures haven't been invented yet. It is hoped that my stories and struggles as a recovering autocrat will be reassuring to others who are trying, on the firing lines, to invent the future of participative management.

Though there are autocratic behaviors that we all share, I'm certain that some of my references to the royal "we" won't fit for everyone. For example, one of my colleagues pointed out that I'm an extrovert while he's an introvert. He's inclined, therefore, to deal differently with his control needs.

I trust that readers will allow me some liberties with the "we's," and will take their own liberties and responsibility for translating my experiences to their own personal circumstances and style.

Finally, I would like to gratefully acknowledge the many friends and clients whose stories appear anonymously throughout the book. In all cases, names and circumstances have been changed to avoid identification and the possibility of offending in any way. It's important for me to add also that when a story is used to illustrate a "negative" example of autocratic behavior, it is offered with a great sense of humility and compassion. There is not one autocratic behavior described in this book that I'm not entirely capable of engaging in myself.

Minneapolis, Minnesota   Richard W. Hallstein
May, 1993

RELIEF FROM BEING IN CHARGE ALL OF THE TIME

Hi. My name is Dick. I'm a recovering autocrat. My life has been one long attempt to gain control of all that is around me. Though I have always tried to use my power for the good of my company, employees, and family, my well-intentioned efforts have often been very trying for my friends and the people in my work life.

One of the confusing things about those of us who are inclined toward autocratic behavior is that often we are very effective and successful people who accomplish a great deal in all aspects of our lives. As a result, it is hard for those people around us to understand or justify the angry feelings that they sometimes feel toward us. It's also hard for us to recognize the need to change.

I have raised three children, been married several times, and worked as a senior executive in a number of U.S. companies. My life inside large corporations spanned twenty-three years. In the past eight years, I have consulted to executives on three continents to help them improve their effectiveness in running their corporations. I have also participated in two long-term men's groups that provide an opportunity for men to learn more about themselves and how to give and get support in their personal and professional lives.

Over the course of these past thirty years, I have discovered that there are many people like myself—people striving for power and control over their lives. We are convinced that if we work hard and smart, we can make anything happen. Worse yet, we believe we *must* make things happen!

We can become addicted to the many, many temporary "highs" that come from believing that we can do anything. The definition of *autocrat* comes from the Greek, meaning "ruling by oneself." No matter what the challenge, we can and must use our personal power to do it ourselves. Others may be involved, but in the end the buck stops here.

This feeling that we are constantly in charge grows in its addictiveness. The more we accomplish the more we're convinced that we can make things happen. We get increasingly addicted to activity, excitement, being in charge, and being successful. We believe that we are a superior kind of human being who can handle anything. Such a burden this can all become!

Sometimes the overwhelming belief that we can and must control everything is brought to a shuddering halt. We confront a problem that even we have to admit is beyond our control; like serious illness, the death of a loved one, or economic downturns leading to job loss or the failure of our business. But we can't cry uncle and admit that it's too big to handle. Why? Because we cannot do that and still hold on to our sense of effectiveness, self-esteem, and worthiness.

This book is offered as a gift to people who want some relief from being in charge all of the time. It is also offered to those who are beginning to realize that the respect and protection formerly afforded by autocracy and authority are gone, or are seriously eroded.

The book is organized into a series of minichapters that can be read either sequentially or randomly. Each chapter represents a special learning from my personal recovery. There are some themes that run throughout and, by necessity, there are some overlaps.

Some of these themes are based on principles taken from the Twelve Steps recovery program. These principles have helped me come to terms with the control issues that interfere with my performance, relationships, and emotional well-being. I've been particularly inspired by the program's constant challenge that I take a regular and fearless inventory of my autocratic behaviors and commit to continuous personal learning and change. Though the program has been a significant source of learning, this book and my recovery do not follow the traditional twelve-step approach. Rather, I draw on a wide range of sources and theories.

Before beginning, I offer a few words of thanks to some of the other spiritual guides that have provided inspiration for my journey: Carl Jung, Joseph Campbell, Carlos Casteñada, George Sheehan, Robert Bly, Merle Fossum, Dan Gable, Robert Fritz, Robert Johnson, M. Scott Peck, and the members of my men's groups.

I am sharing my personal recovery not because I'm recovered, but because I'm recovering—and I hope that in the pages that follow managers, partners, and parents will find support for leading more joyous, manageable, and effective lives.

CHAPTER ONE

ONCE BEGUN, THE JOURNEY NEVER ENDS

As we begin to examine our autocratic behaviors, we would be wise to be gentle and generous with ourselves. It is very natural to try to use our personal power to bring order to our lives. The human experience is characterized by this yearning to feel less vulnerable in a universe that can seem quite chaotic.

A sense of chaos and unmanageableness has been increasing in recent years. Things often seem out of control. This can lead to anger, discouragement, and doubt about our effectiveness in all aspects of our lives. In turn, it may spark a response to redouble our efforts to gain control.

To begin a journey toward a more peaceable and productive relationship with the world around us, we must ultimately yield to the fact that much of life is indeed beyond our control. People, competition, markets, and business cycles, to name a few examples, cannot readily be controlled by any individual.

This recognition brings us to a turning point that is likely to trigger some understandable fear. Much of what we have learned about living and managing comes under question. In addition, deeper acknowledgment of our personal fears and doubts is often new territory. Feeling such fears for the first time leads to a fear of feeling fearful! This can bring on bouts of uncertainty and cause us to doubt our toughness, courage, and ability to make decisions. Again, this is very unfamiliar territory for many of us.

Although it may seem unimaginable at first, the recognition that much of life is being driven by forces beyond our control can be a great relief, relieving us of the burden of being in charge of everything. However, we are still left with the difficult task of learning new ways to live and manage within the limits of our personal power and control.

It has taken me many years to turn to others for help and support in dealing with these fears, uncertainties, and problems. It seems so logical that the more scary and difficult the problems, the more benefit we would gain from seeking help in finding solutions. Yet, I can report that I have been dragged reluctantly to this realization. As a matter of fact, I constantly struggle with the feeling that somehow I will have less vulnerability and more control if I do it myself.

It is true that life can feel less messy if we don't involve others in helping to solve our problems and deal with our uncertainties. It's also true that handling matters on our own allows us to respond quickly. And this, in turn, can cause us to have a temporary belief that we're on top of things.

Increasingly my new sense of power, self-control, and certainty is coming from a vastly expanded feeling of optimism and passion for dramatically increasing the involvement of a wide range of people in helping to deal with issues at work and in my personal life. I've come to believe that any gains that flow from my more autocratic and controlling behaviors are offset by losses in new potential and possibilities that come from limiting the participation of others.

Whatever effectiveness I've gained in realizing the potential that exists in all situations has come from the discovery that I need more and more eyes to look at everything. This is the only way that I can develop a deep sense of what's going on and what needs to be done. Further, it's the only way that I can bolster my personal confidence and not be crippled by the indecisiveness that comes from a growing recognition of the complexities involved in many of the decisions I'm facing.

To create a climate of participation and sustain a commitment to it, I have had to develop a value for it, a vision of it, and a constant dialogue about it.

The stories included in this book are my best retrospective explanation of how I came to develop a *value* for participation and partnership, how my experiences painted pictures of a *vision* of shared responsibility that inspires me daily to new experiments, and how I'm trying to keep the *dialogue* about the topic alive so as to offset my considerable ongoing natural momentum to retreat to more familiar autocratic behaviors.

The stories are meant to be more like poems than prescriptions. My hope is that you will read them with an eye toward creating your own personal values, vision, and dialogue about participation and respectful partnering.

I have found no instant fixes. Just when I think I've mastered my tendencies toward autocratic behaviors, they pop up again. Just when I think I've found the right mix of personal control and participation with others, I discover that it didn't work, and I need to go back to the drawing board.

Once begun, the journey never ends.

On one particularly discouraging occasion, I was complaining to my therapist that I wished I had learned a certain lesson earlier. With no hesitation he responded, "That's about the time in life that we learn that lesson."

Some of what we have to learn will just come with time. Not a comforting thought for the autocratic part of us that seeks instant gratification and closure. Yet, the important thing is that we are on the journey.

Sometimes I waste a lot of energy wishing that others would change and make it easier for me. If the truth be known, I not only wish that they would change, I often find myself demanding or forcefully "encouraging" such change. Needless to say, there is a place for coaching and supporting others' growth. However, I've come to place more faith in focusing most of my energy on my own development. And, to my great surprise, my own change has spontaneously brought about many desired changes in others.

What's the payoff for this long and arduous journey?

Our rewards will come from how we feel and perform. We will feel more human and less lonely because we are more connected to all those around us. We will become more creative and decisive because we will have participative processes that bring out the grand potential in all situations. Our lessened self-importance will offer great relief from the burdens of being in charge of everything. And we will see others achieve their full potential in response to our changing behaviors.

Finally, if we reach out to other recovering autocrats, we'll discover that we're not alone on this journey, which will allow us to unburden ourselves and learn from one another. This book is my personal attempt at such outreach. I am enthusiastically anticipating the quantum leaps in my own development that can come from your responses to my stories.

I welcome you to the journey and cherish the opportunity to share my memoirs with you.

CHAPTER TWO

A POWER GREATER
THAN MYSELF

Years ago a boss and I were discussing some business results that were not going very well. As is often the case, the conversation turned quickly to accusations that more could have been done to ensure results. I found myself vacillating between defending my performance and experiencing vague feelings of shame for not having met expectations. In a fit of frustration I lashed out with a fishing analogy to make my point. (Strange what we'll do under stress—I know little about fishing!) I said, "You can't make the fish jump on the hook! You can investigate and find the right stream, get the finest equipment, use the most appealing bait, and fish at the right time of day. Yet, some days the fish just don't bite! You can't make the fish jump on the hook!"

My boss, without batting an eye, said, "Yes, you can make the fish jump on the hook! No matter how hard you think you've tried, if it didn't work, it wasn't enough!"

At first, I was flabbergasted at this outrageous point of

view. Then, it began to dawn on me that I led my own life as though "the rule" were true. It was a shocking realization that my boss's rule was "Dick's rule." I completely believed the old adage, "Where there's a will, there's a way." No wonder my life-long addiction to willfulness.

Later, my boss and I had some long discussions about this rule that we both seemed to have woven so destructively into our expectations for ourselves and others. As we untangled the web of issues and beliefs behind the rule, a large, mutually-held fear came into view: if we let go of the belief that "where there's a will, there's a way," how could we be certain that we and others could be counted on to do everything possible at all times? Would we stop being responsible if we believed that a power greater than ourselves could control the outcome?

After more thought, a new perception took hold: what we really have as human beings is responsibility, not power! At first, this didn't seem fair. In the world of work, we have always believed that you don't give people responsibility without the commensurate power.

Then it struck me that maybe this whole idea of our alleged power and control has just been a "useful lie," a way to make certain that we show up every day. Perhaps the myth of our own power is really more unbelievable than a belief in a higher power that many find so intellectually unacceptable. What might it be like to believe in a power greater than myself? Since my own control is increasingly shown to be a fantasy, and traditional religious beliefs are so hard to accept, what's the answer? If I were to stop being "my own higher power," what could I turn myself over to? If I correct the illusion of my control, what will be my source of energy and hope? How will I motivate myself and others?

I found myself up against a very difficult edge. Perhaps you have been there too. Even if we would like to be relieved of responsibility for everything, it may be hard to imagine a higher power in which we can believe and take comfort.

Several years ago I found myself attending a Christmas service at a local Catholic church. (Christmas services at Catholic churches seem to be a tradition for many people raised as Christians, even if they're now nonbelievers.) The service included a wonderful one-woman show. The woman enacted a story in which she assumed the role of the mother of Mary, the mother of Jesus. As the story unfolds, Mary's mother is faced with a terrible decision. Is she willing to believe her daughter's incredible story that she is pregnant but has not been sexually involved? Mary's mother is the first one to confront the virgin birth story. Can you imagine dealing with such a preposterous story from your daughter?

While listening to the internal dialogue of Mary's mother, for reasons that I do not entirely understand, I finally got clear about the many "unbelievable" stories found in all religions.

13

These stories present us with the fundamental faith question: will we believe in something we can't explain? The stories are metaphors to test our capacity to submit to something greater than ourselves. It doesn't really make much difference which story we use as our faith test—the virgin birth, the resurrection of Christ, or countless stories from other religions.

Unfortunately, our humble human attempts to create stories that explain our relationship to the unknown and unknowable often distract us from coming to grips with the real issue that there is something greater than ourselves. This feeds our fantasy of "ruling by ourselves," giving rise to the willful, autocratic belief that we can explain the unexplainable and control the uncontrollable in ourselves and others.

So, the case I'm submitting for your consideration is this: we can't make the fish jump on the hook. Where there is a will, there is *not* always a way. And unless we can develop a deep sense of a power greater than us, we will continue to make ourselves and others crazy. Further, I suggest the additional hypothesis that understanding our powerlessness and lack of control is the most direct path to unleashing the full power in ourselves and others! It's a wonderful paradox.

What does it look like to live with this paradox? How does it affect our lives? How does it change our relationships? What is the effect on our experiences at work? How will it feel not to be in control?

First of all, we must begin by acknowledging that most of what we are is a total gift from an unimaginable power! We arrived here on this planet with certain God-given talents, physical capabilities, and life circumstances, which are a gift. In addition, each new day on this earth is a gift.

At times I find myself stunned by the simplicity of this learning. When I am out taking my morning run by the lake, I think, "I could have been a duck!" There, but for the grace of a higher power, go I. I laugh at this little joke, but at a very important level I am overpowered by awareness of the gift of my unique existence. I find it very hard to hold on to my misplaced pride and arrogance when I acknowledge the unexplainable origin of my good fortune of having been given another day on this earth.

It can be quite a risk to be so grateful. Terror often sits right around the corner from gratitude. It takes a great deal of courage to face our daily affairs feeling grateful rather than powerful. Yet, it is worth it. People in our lives will soon begin to experience a qualitative difference in dealing with our gratefulness instead of our power. Our lack of self-importance will be noticed and cherished. And all of this just from developing a deep understanding that but for the grace of your higher power, you could have been a duck!

As we go deeper on this journey to rid ourselves of Don Quixote-like patterns of heroism, other joys are waiting for us.

For example, as we let go of our omnipotence, we are much less critical of ourselves and others. When things don't go as planned, we start feeling more curious rather than judgmental. We still wonder and explore what we could have done. But the emotional tone of our investigation is much more friendly— both toward ourselves and others with whom we are engaged.

In the world of work, our informal and formal appraisals of people become less of a report card and more of a mutually-explored attempt to agree on what we can do something about and what is beyond our control. We strive together to have the wisdom and courage to know the difference.

As we go forward experimenting with this powerless/ powerful paradox, we discover that something inside of us that needed to die is dying. Having corrected the illusion of our control, we begin to live by the pure energy of gratefulness.

CHAPTER THREE

THE CASE FOR INCOMPETENCE

We can become very invested in always knowing the answer. We often require that those working for us know all the answers, too. Not knowing the answer is a very serious matter for those of us who are striving to stay in control.

Because we feel compelled to stay on top of things, we face some tremendous obstacles. Examined in the full light of day, it could cause us to wonder if we are up to the challenge. For example, it is reported that the pace of change is five times what it was fifty years ago! Others say that everything there is to know is doubling every seven years.

I find myself overwhelmed at times by the information age. There are so many books to be read. Magazines flood my office and home. My daughter, who is pursuing a doctoral degree in the same field as I work in, talks about books and theories that I haven't even heard of. When I go to conferences or seminars, I hear about other essential learning experiences that I "must" attend.

As for my office in-basket, I find myself developing

creative systems to shift piles of "must" reading from my desk to my briefcase and back again. Sometimes, to my great shame, because the incoming information flow has overtaken me, I seek relief by throwing away the most outdated things that I haven't read. As I pitch the unread journals and other communications in the wastebasket, I do so with great fear that I may be missing something vital. Fact is, I probably am! I've actually come to believe that in today's world if you think you know what you need to know, you probably don't really "get it." In the nineties, it's no longer possible to stay current. It's no longer possible to truly keep pace with all that we need to know.

Maintaining an aura of phony expertise is very trying. Many of us feel at great risk, however, of letting others know that we don't know something. Our fears come from growing up in a culture in which it's not wise to look confused or uncertain. Increasingly, our self-esteem gets tied to being right. As the world swirls around us and we are barraged with information and change, we hide our uncertainty and feelings of vulnerability.

Several years ago I was asked to help the executives of a division of a large bank develop a strategic plan. Before taking them off-site for a three-day planning session, I interviewed each of them to get some insights into the issues they felt a need to address in the strategic plan. One by one, all the executives told me that they were very unclear about the future of their business. They were facing dramatic changes in legislation, competition, and technology.

On the first day of the planning session, I began by feeding back to them the areas of their business that required some strategic rethinking, based on what they had told me in the private interviews. My intention was to use the feedback as a vehicle to set the agenda for the next three days. As I began to list the issues they had described in the interviews, the boss started to challenge each item by protesting to the group, "We sure as hell better know what we're doing in [this or that] area."

It wasn't long before everyone began to fall in line and deny any sense of uncertainty about any of the strategic issues. It suddenly was apparent to all of the executives in the room that if they could just get their subordinates to perform at a higher level and get the corporation to give them more money to fund their operations, all would be well!

I was astounded at this renewal of confidence and certainty on the part of all the participants. It became clear that if they were to continue to deny their concerns, we didn't have a chance of making any strategic breakthroughs. Such breakthroughs only occur when people admit they're confused and uncertain.

I decided to take a risk and confront them with their denial of the information given privately in advance of the meeting. To get their attention, I introduced the concept of how difficult it is to feel competent in the face of the present-day explosion of knowledge and information.

To my amazement, there was a collective sigh of relief from everyone—even the boss! The opportunity to speak honestly about their fears and feelings of uncertainty released an incredible burst of energy and comradery.

Leaping at the opportunity, I created a wall chart I labeled the "Incompetence Manifesto." The document read as follows: "We the leadership team of the X department declare that we have no idea what our strategy for the future should be. Since we are very capable and committed people individually and collectively, if we continue to admit our ignorance, there is a very good chance that we will be able to determine a good course for the future. Admitting what we don't know is our best ally and source of creativity for inventing our future." Everyone then ceremoniously paraded to the chart and boldly affixed his or her signature to it.

The planning session that followed produced exciting new thinking, some marvelous relationships among the team members, and several very important strategies to engage in long-term processes to get smart about what they needed to learn.

I find that being part of a community of people who are willing to admit to one another what they don't know can be very satisfying and supportive. This collective comfort with our "incompetence" has enormous potential to keep us energized and focused on discovering and acquiring the learning we need to ensure our constant renewal and growth. In one case, some colleagues and I, who were stumbling for the first time through the painful learnings associated with running a small business, developed a motto for ourselves which read, "We don't stay dumb long!" This helped us be more gentle with each other about our inadequacies and mistakes, and it also signaled our intention and commitment to accelerated and continuous learning.

As part of an overall strategy to create a learning culture in his organization, a client of mine put signs on all the cafeteria tables that read, "What have you learned today?" The same question was even printed at the bottom of the company writing pads used by employees every day to send notes to each other. Many update meetings also began by asking, "What have you learned since we were last together?"

Some might experience such signs and slogans as somewhat contrived. Nevertheless, any invitation to share what we're learning is by implication an affirmation that we're not expected to know it all. I believe that using any method possible to release ourselves and others from the need to appear competent at all times can contribute handsomely to our mutual success, sanity and, ironically, the pace of our learning.

CHAPTER FOUR

CASTING LIGHT ON OUR DARK SIDE

When we feel a sense of powerlessness or lack of control, we can get very angry. This anger is often accompanied by an aura of superiority and arrogance.

Some of the more extreme examples of our anger can be seen in our relationships with people in service roles like waitresses and waiters, salespeople in retail stores, and receptionists. These are people over whom we can "lord" our power. They become particularly attractive targets when a bad week at the office makes us feel out of control. We may feel at risk if we explode at the office, so we release our dark side elsewhere.

Several years ago my wife and I stopped to pick up a number of items at a drugstore. We had been out to dinner earlier and were both anxious to get done and get home after a hard day at the office.

Deciding to divide and conquer, we each grabbed shopping carts and went our separate ways with our shopping agendas confirmed. After gathering quite a few of my assigned items, I realized that I needed to go to the bathroom. Pushing my nearly full shopping cart, I wandered back to the pharmacist to ask to use the rest room.

Before going on with this story, I must explain that I had become quite an expert at intimidating unsuspecting service people into letting me use their rest rooms. It had been my experience that because of potential vandalism many small store owners and retailers do not want to let the public use the stores' rest rooms.

As I approached the pharmacist, I was prepared with a number of strategies to get my way. I would first be polite in my request. If that met a deaf ear, I could offer some veiled legal threats (I never did really find out what responsibilities a store owner has to provide public rest rooms, but it made for a good argument). As a last resort, I could always lash out with the promise that failure to let me use the rest room would result in a loss of my considerable business forever.

In my intense mental preparation for the upcoming encounter with the pharmacist, my compulsive plans to ensure that I would have control of the situation were on high alert. It was essential that I have all my bases covered.

I approached the pharmacist and asked politely, "May I use your rest room?"

He replied, "We don't have a rest room."

"Are you telling me that you don't have a rest room or are

you telling me that I can't use your rest room?" I asked.

"We don't have a rest room for you to use," he said, cleverly avoiding my actual question.

I can't tell you precisely what happened next. Something exploded inside me.

"You lying son of a bitch," I said. "Of course you have a rest room! You may not want me to use your rest room, but don't tell me you don't have one, you lying bastard!"

I banged my shopping cart dramatically on the floor and pranced toward the exit. As I was leaving, I shouted over my shoulder, "You've lost my business forever, and I'm going to tell all my friends to stop shopping here!"

My wife was standing nearby and, to her great dismay, witnessed my outburst. Without saying a word, she paid for her purchases and followed me out the door.

The discussion that followed was difficult. I tried unsuccessfully to convince her that I was justified in my actions. She rejected my attempts to rationalize my behavior, insisting that my rage was inappropriate for the circumstances. After a while, I began to see her point and started to develop feelings of guilt and shame about the incident.

Over the next few days I realized that even though the incident at the drugstore was an extreme example, it wasn't an isolated occurrence. It was becoming clear to me that a part of me was out of control, which was quite disturbing. Once you come to this realization, you are forced either to choose to let part of yourself be out of control or do something about it. It can't be ignored.

A visit to my therapist came next.

In the months ahead we began to uncover a number of behaviors at work and at home that seemed to roar up out of some dark place when my sense of control or power was threatened. In one session a particularly significant break-through occurred.

We were discussing a troubling incident where I had become verbally abusive to a woman. In the middle of the story, my therapist stopped me and asked, "Did you get aroused when you were yelling at her? Some of my clients do." I was stopped dead! The question flabbergasted and disgusted me.

Overcoming my shock and disgust took a number of further sessions. As time went by, my therapist helped me open up to the understanding that wielding my power could be quite stimulating: that I really liked having power! I certainly didn't like being "caught" with my desire for power and control showing, but the fact remained that I enjoyed being in control…having power over others.

Being confronted with my enjoyment of power has been shocking, somewhat frightening, and in some ways shameful. It's like looking at a part of yourself that's been amputated. However, I've come to believe that the more we deny these things in ourselves, the more they are in control of us. The less we understand our dark sides (and the secret enjoyment they bring us), the more likely they are to come roaring out to surprise us and others.

The temptation to call on our dark side to help us feel more secure in this increasingly insecure world is quite normal. For recovering autocrats like myself, however, the addictive magnetism toward our dark sides can at times feel quite unmanageable.

Recovery from this addiction constantly uncovers surprising paradoxes. As we conduct a fearless inventory, we discover some alarming polarities within us. We begin to see our capacity for love and hate, for nourishing and abusing; and we acknowledge that we deeply cherish the dark sides of these polarities.

Acknowledging that we are not always "on the side of the angels" can be very disconcerting. Worse yet, we are forced to abandon our myth that our intentions are always good, even if we make mistakes. Our intentions aren't always good!

When we accept this shadow side of ourselves, we make a permanent break with the idea of our own perfection. Relieving ourselves of this burden of perfection is accompanied by substantial further relief from guilt and shame. If we readily accept our imperfection, we're not so surprised when we see evidence of it. Further, we don't need to be so defensive when we get caught with our imperfections showing, which helps us avoid addictive spirals into further crazy behavior to cover our mistakes and regain control.

The point I wish to stress here is that *recognition of the problem does not make it disappear.* It simply becomes more manageable as we develop a relationship with these paradoxical parts of ourselves.

Carl Jung likens it to two people sitting down to get to the bottom of a problem. In the discussions between the "two people" inside each of us, we recognize that we can't control these separate parts. They can, however, have a living relationship with each other. They can engage in a continuous dialogue. They can accept, oppose, or reject certain behaviors.

Recognizing that we can have such internal discussions helps us realize the full extent of our responsibility. This recognition is the source of whatever real power we have in life.

Admitting to those around us that we are struggling with these parts of ourselves can be another source of power and intimacy. Bringing our struggle with our dark sides into the light of day can be very healing for us and all of those in our personal and professional lives. It's much easier for people to be empathetic, generous, and forgiving when they are experiencing the struggling part versus the superior part of us.

In my own journey, I've come to believe that my effectiveness in all aspects of my life is most dependent on what I know about myself—not on what I know about others or organization politics, not even on my professional competency.

I find this internal journey to take far more courage than any of my forays into corporate problems. Yet, to my considerable surprise and joy, my successes in managing myself have brought me far more success than all of my past attempts at managing others.

CHAPTER FIVE

STRUGGLES WITH SELF-IMPORTANCE

It can be a serious problem when we believe everything we are doing is vitally important. Work can be a particularly powerful source of reinforcement of this myth.

Superior efforts on our part often bring great rewards. Some of us end up with fancy titles and impressive offices and salaries that allow us to purchase a never-ending array of things that support our feelings of self-importance. I'm certain that making a lot of money isn't the only way to achieve an undue sense of grandiosity. However, it can present a serious threat to a balanced perspective concerning our importance in the universe.

When I was a teenager, I began to suspect that maybe I and, for that matter, all human beings weren't as important as we thought we were. As an expression of this emerging discovery, I wrote a short story for my high school English class. In the story, a young man invented the world's most powerful microscope. He put a drop of water on a slide and gazed into the microscope. To his amazement, he discovered another world in the drop of water. In this other world he saw an incredibly beautiful and wonderful young woman and fell madly in love with her.

I won't bore you with the details of my sophomore English paper, but I would like you to know how the story ended: the drop of water evaporated!

I was so pleased with myself. In this simple story I felt I had captured the lonely, unexplainable mystery of humankind's existence. Our whole world is like a drop of water in the universe—a drop of water that could disappear at any moment. A tiny drop of water whose insignificance is beyond our comprehension.

Though my official posture about this discovery was one of fearless rationality, I've come to realize that in that story I had actually confronted a fear that shaped much of my behavior for the next twenty years. Since the whole universe was fundamentally unexplainable, whatever meaning there was to be was for me to make. I had to figure it out. It was up to me.

Presenting this bravado and supreme sense of personal responsibility was much easier and more socially acceptable than crying out in despair as I stared into the empty impersonal universe. Many rewards accompanied my bravado. My primary source of reward and meaning came from obtaining the approval of admiring bosses, coworkers, friends, and family members.

It took me a long time to understand that to have a sense of meaning primarily driven by approval meant losing my identity. I did not exist except as I was approved of by others. Therefore, any threats to my success or approval were a threat to my essential sense of meaning.

I suppose it's possible to go through life convinced that our successes are the source of life's meaning. However, I must report that as I reached mid-life, it became increasingly difficult not to question once more the ultimate meaning of my life in the context of the universe.

A personal illness or a professional failure may prompt that question. Or we might accidentally revisit the question by reading or hearing something that causes us to have new concerns about the fundamental significance of our existence. I remember how empty and sad I felt when a friend innocently told me she had read that very few people can remember anything about anyone in their family beyond their grandparents. In fact, many don't even know much about their grandparents.

Another melancholy moment came when my most successful friend recently confided to me that no matter what he accomplishes, he never really feels satisfied. He often wonders to himself, Is this all there is?

Thus, I came to a point in my life where I was no longer certain that my personal successes had meaning. Driving myself in pursuit of approval had caused me and others considerable heartache—and the successes felt hollow. It was becoming clear that my fame was fleeting and temporal.

Here I was undeniably faced with the inevitability that I too would be ashes. I was face-to-face with the possibility that what I had accomplished may not have been important. In my "responsible" lifelong attempt to create meaning, did some meaning slip past me?

In facing these questions and dilemmas, I discovered an approach that has helped me make some different choices about what is important in my life and has also helped me keep my personal sense of importance in better perspective. This way of viewing the world has somewhat mysteriously shifted the center of my ego to things greater than myself— be they ever so unexplainable.

The simple secret is that I regularly submit my struggles with self-importance and meaning to the tombstone test! For example, when I am feeling enormous tension to ensure that something "vital" I'm working on doesn't fail, I ask myself, If I died today, would I want this last accomplishment on my tombstone?

When I'm feeling a particular need to gain someone's approval, I ask myself, If I died today, would I want the fact that this person admired me to appear on my tombstone?

When I'm engaged in a win/lose debate with an important colleague, I ask myself, If I die today, do I want my tombstone to read, "Here lies Dick. On the last day of his life he won a ferocious debate."

It might not surprise you to know that my answer to many of these questions is "No!" Very often I'm surprised to find how little attachment I have to many of these things—to which I might have given great meaning—when I submit them to this test.

I suspect that many of us have some fear that if we lived regularly with death so present in our consciousness, we might not be willing to "show up" each day. We would live for the moment and become irresponsible. In essence, we don't trust ourselves with our inability to understand the true meaning of life. There is also a fear that if we all begin to speak the truth about how unclear we are about the significance of these worldly matters, nobody could be counted on to be responsible. Is it any wonder, then, that these fears sometimes drive us toward falsely inflating the importance of our undertakings and imposing ever tighter control on ourselves and others?

Here again I confront another paradox. It was only when I acknowledged my inability to understand my meaning in the context of the universe that I was released to *find* meaning and reduce my overdeveloped sense of importance. I succumbed to "the mystery." I admitted that I had absolutely no idea what my purpose is here on earth. Further, it seemed that every human being who preceded me on this planet was as incapable as I am of making meaning of this. We are all in this together! All on equal ground. All part of a great holy mystery: the powerful and the poor, the educated and the simple, those from the fifth century B.C. or the twenty-first century A.D., those from the first world or the third world. No one has an advantage in the search for purpose and meaning.

How differently the day begins when we start with a deep sense of mystery, awe, and oneness with others, rather than feeling superior and driven to accumulate more points on an artificially contrived score card of life.

But, holding on to a sense of mystery, awe, and oneness instead of pride and self-importance can be very difficult. Here's an example.

Several years ago, as part of my recovery, I sought and found a new church to attend. To my pleasure, the church had a great music program. Every Sunday the sanctuary swelled with the one thousand voices in the congregation. I love to sing! What's more, I sing quite well. So every Sunday I stood in the congregation and lifted my voice to the heavens. At the end of the service, it became quite routine for a nearby parishioner to stop and tell me how much he or she enjoyed sitting near me and hearing me sing. Though I always made some modest comment, if the truth be known, I was quite proud of myself and enjoyed the adulation.

As the Sundays came and went, I found myself thinking

more and more about my singing. If good songs were selected that I could harmonize to, I belted out my part and waited for the praise to follow. If the song selections did not suit me, I was disappointed at not getting a chance to perform. Interestingly enough, I was very aware of how my pride was interfering with my spiritual journey, but I was unable to let go of my desire for attention and admiration.

One Sunday we were standing and joining our voices in a particularly rousing chorus when I stopped singing and began looking around the congregation. One by one, I took them in: a very old man, who could hardly stand, barely moving his lips; a young black boy, with his adopted white parents, appearing distracted by his younger white stepsister; a lesbian couple holding hands, singing and smiling regularly and lovingly at each other; a tall, well-dressed businessman unable to carry a tune.

Suddenly I was struck by my connection to all these people. Tears came to my eyes as I imagined their lives, joys, and struggles. I was overcome with an awareness of how my pride and performance addiction had been interfering with my connection to these other human beings. Every Sunday I had been missing an incredible opportunity to have a meaningful experience with kindred souls, all on a shared exploration of life's mysteries. I had been trying to outsing them instead of listening and appreciating the many other songs around me.

What a metaphor for my life!

Painful as it is, I have come to revel in discoveries such as these. I've found that constantly "living in the shadow of my tombstone," regularly sharing the unexplainable "Holy Mysteries" with others, and beginning each day with a sense of awe and oneness with others makes the questions about the meaning of my life seem themselves meaningless.

CHAPTER SIX

THE COURAGE FOR NECESSARY MESSES

Many of us feel a very strong need for rules and guarantees. Rules and guarantees provide us with a sense of comfort and control. We have an intense desire to predict the outcome of everything in which we are engaged. We don't like things to be messy.

At work, we excel in our creative pursuit of strategies to cover all options. These admirable characteristics often bring us great recognition and reward. At home, we attempt to add the firm hand of clarity and order to all matters of importance to our families. It is not uncommon for others—at work and at home—to wait for us to make final decisions on important issues.

It is easy to confuse this deferential treatment on the part of family members and work associates with respect for our wisdom. Yet, I'm convinced that their behavior is often more attributable to fear. They may indeed respect our apparent clarity and mastery of all situations, small and great. But their respect is accompanied by fear of the consequences of making a move without our approval.

Work associates and family members have particularly strong aversions to approaching us about matters that seem messy, unclear, or ambiguous. They expect us either to deny the problem or respond in one of the following ways: 1) we will have a strong opinion on the subject and will infer that they should have understood the rules governing the particular situation; 2) we will make a decision to create order on the spot, and they will have to live with it; or 3) we will not know what to do and that will make us defensive (a mask for being scared). In the latter case, it's hard to predict what our behavior will be. We do know that it's not a pretty sight when we start to feel scared and out of control.

A friend of mine was having great difficulty in her marriage. We had many conversations in which she stated that she would have to leave the marriage unless her husband was willing to go to therapy and work on their problems. On many occasions I encouraged my friend to talk to her husband and let him know how serious the situation had become for her. However, she kept saying, "I have no confidence that I can talk to him in a way that will ensure he will go to therapy with me. As a matter of fact, I'm convinced that he will be mad at me and may even leave me if I pressure him to go to therapy."

There is a sad ending to this story. My friend did not

pressure her husband to go to therapy and, within a year's time, she left him! An ironic completion to her self-fulfilling prophecy. My friend (a confirmed control freak) gave up whatever power she could have had in this situation by not engaging her husband in a difficult conversation. She didn't know the "rules" for conducting such a messy dialogue and she couldn't guarantee the outcome in advance!

While there is certainly no guarantee that conversations would have produced the desired results, it's fairly certain that no conversation will produce undesirable results.

This pattern of avoiding messy confrontations is not limited to the powerless, weak of heart, or unskilled. Many powerful people frequently avoid confrontations like these because they're least familiar and least comfortable with being out of control.

I understand the fears that stop us from wading into these messy, unpredictable situations for which there are no rules or guarantees. On the other hand, I can report from personal experiences that courageous steps into the unknown have significant potential to create new levels of problem solving, mutual respect, understanding, and intimacy in all of our relationships, at home and at work.

In the workplace, managers often work hard to clarify what they expect from their staffs. The best of these managers spend considerable time defining strategy, clarifying financial objectives, and articulating the values that should be used to guide decision making. These plans, strategies, and the like are much like the Constitution of the United States. We spend a great deal of time carefully crafting each word in the document, then we must spend the rest of eternity arguing over whether or not what we are doing is "constitutional." Nothing is certain, and this leads to constant debate about every nuance and interpretation. Competent people of sound mind and good intentions have passionate discussions and disagreements over what is meant by what is written in the Constitution.

This is very dangerous territory for recovering autocrats. Our best-laid plans cannot protect us from ambiguity, uncertainty, and uncomfortable levels of personal involvement. We must constantly submit ourselves to challenges by others. Worse yet, if we are honest with ourselves, we have to admit that in spite of our clear plans, we often do not know for certain what we ought to be doing about a particular mess.

The parallels between the dilemmas we face when wading into messy, unpredictable personal conversations and those we face when broaching incredibly difficult attempts to translate, live, and make meaning of our company plans become clear. We can no longer take comfort in our ability to establish guidelines or directions that will provide a certain path through the hazards that lie ahead.

In all matters, we must rely less and less on knowing

what to say and do. We must rely more and more on our courage, ability, and willingness to go forward when we and others aren't entirely certain where the path is leading.

We must shift our emphasis from relying on our abilities to plan, organize, motivate, and control to developing our capability and appetite for messy engagement with all of those with whom we interact.

CHAPTER SEVEN

A BIAS FOR NO ACTION

An addiction to action is very common in our frenetic world. We are always busy, busy, busy! We seem to be compelled to do something, whether or not it's needed.

There is a sense that we are in constant hand-to-hand combat with the world around us. We are prepared (compelled) to lend a hand to everyone within range of our influence. It doesn't seem to really matter whether the problem is large or small, important or unimportant, our concern or someone else's concern—we stand ready to take action! We are convinced that if we offer a little of our wisdom and experience to any situation, it will be given a push in the right direction. We have totally bought into the adage that there are three kinds of people in the world: those who make things happen, those who watch things happen, and those who wonder what the hell happened.

To illustrate how pervasive this sense that the world needs us always on duty can be, let me admit that for many years I worried about what my friends would do at parties when

I wasn't there to keep things moving! Clearly, though my bias for action was perhaps admirable, my addiction to action was quite neurotic. It's not just that I was willing to act; the fact is that I was not willing to not act. I paid a high personal price for my addiction to action.

It's exhausting to go through each day feeling responsible for taking action to further all projects, catch all mistakes, get all the misguided back on track, and attack all perceived injustices. At work, at home, in restaurants, on airplanes, and at little league games, nothing was too large or too small or too unimportant for my attention.

The information about the effect of type A (autocratic) behavior on health and longevity is widely known. One redeeming factor about type A's is that because they are so compulsively busy, they rarely stop long enough to notice how their body is feeling. Thus, they often drop dead without the troublesome difficulty of dealing with distracting warning signals.

Another result of constant busyness is that there is little time wasted on idle reflection. There is not much chance that autocrats will be caught with their feet up on their desks gazing blankly out the window. In fact, a common complaint of autocrats is that they don't have enough time to think. When this complaint is being registered, the listener has the distinct impression that the speaker is quite proud of this fact. It's as though a measure of importance and success is that you don't have time to think.

Since there was no time or perceived value for reflection or thinking, I found myself leaping from one task to another, unencumbered by learnings from past experiences. Thus, when I made mistakes, I often repeated them. This observation was rather disturbing in light of one definition of mental illness: a condition in which we continue to repeat behaviors even though we know they will result in an unwanted outcome.

In addition to the personal consequences of my excessive bias for action, I was equally disturbed by a growing realization that my constant interventions did not leave space for others to show what they were capable of doing. I was shocked to discover how well parties went without me. To my dismay, I've even discovered that some parties go better without me. Clearly, there are people who flourish at these parties when some of the spotlight that I had commanded becomes available to them.

This learning was forcefully endorsed for me when I became involved in some research that had interesting implications about what happens when people in positions of power aren't around to excessively meddle. We were asked to look at the impact of not quickly filling openings for store manager positions. The study was intended to show how store performance suffered when there was no manager in place for two or three months. The study had been commissioned by those responsible for recruiting store managers. It was their hope that the results would support their request for additional resources to do a better job of filling these vacancies more quickly. To our amazement, there was a consistent improvement in store performance during the two to three months that it took to restaff the position!

I'm not suggesting that long-term performance would be enhanced by eliminating store managers. Nevertheless, it is provocative to imagine what kinds of changes could occur if we would thoughtfully step aside and make space on life's stage for others to more easily come into the spotlight.

Another lesson I learned about the consequences of my constant pushing is that people don't like to be pushed around! Much of the resistance to our autocratic behavior is a reaction to our constant interventions in the affairs of others. After a while, it doesn't matter what our intentions are or whether we're right, people simply want us to back off and let them act on their own.

There is one set of circumstances where a bias for action is entirely stalemated. This has to do with those situations where there is nothing anyone can do. For example, when a loved one suffers a serious illness, the primary support that can be offered is "being there" for the person. Being versus doing is very unfamiliar territory. We would be very skilled at rallying to find the best medical treatment available for our ailing friend. But when action is not where it's at, we're often at a loss as to what to do.

These are "not doing" behaviors that action junkies find difficult to learn; they are receptive rather than expressive behaviors. They include listening and empathizing. As an example, I've been reminded at times that I have two ears and one mouth, which is a gentle hint regarding the frequency with which I deploy these capabilities.

Though I've learned over the years that there are many circumstances where no action on my part is in order, for someone who has been engaged in lifelong hand-to-hand combat, this can seem like surrender. As I've experimented with the more receptive behaviors, however, I've added more versatility to my responses to various life situations. With some "not doing" successes behind me, a new vision of the future has emerged. This vision has me seeking at all times to use the least action required to be effective. What a relief for all concerned!

CHAPTER EIGHT

NOURISHING THE SPIRIT

It's not unusual to feel a profound sense of concern when passing out words of approval. It's almost as though we are afraid that our praise will lessen the tension required for high levels of performance. We sometimes behave as though we are surrounded by people who must be regularly reminded of the consequences of poor performance. Creating this tension seems like a reliable method of accomplishing our desired outcomes. On the other hand, letting up on people feels rather hazardous.

Forty years ago management literature started to extol the virtues of Theory Y versus Theory X to guide our management practices. Loosely interpreted, Theory Y said that we could count on people to be responsible, self-motivated, and committed to the greater good. The Theory Y assumptions about human behavior disavowed the prevailing Theory X assumptions that human beings could not be counted on to behave in a responsible, self-managing, and committed manner.

During the intervening four decades we have not made a

great deal of progress in overcoming our fear of interacting with people in a way that reflects a serious belief in Theory Y assumptions. Command and control techniques continue to prevail. Unfortunately, the collective impact of decades of management practices that have tried to control "untrustworthy" employees by sheer dominance has left its scars. Today there are large numbers of seriously alienated and disenfranchised people in the work world—at all levels! Many people feel angry and disempowered; as a result, they often give much, much less than they are capable of giving.

I'm reminded of a story about fleas. Apparently, mature fleas are capable of jumping twenty feet in the air. However, if they are hatched and raised in a box with a lid on it, when the lid is removed, they never jump to the levels of their innate capability.

Our longstanding degree of mistrust, combined with a highly disenfranchised work force, creates a very dangerous set of circumstances. It's becoming evident that much of what we want to accomplish will be impossible unless we can get all those around us to enroll enthusiastically in the challenges we face. Unfortunately, we're not at all confident that we can count on folks to do their part. To make matters worse, many alienated employees are behaving in ways that justify our concerns.

Historically, the response to this dilemma has been to become even more demanding and to clarify the consequences awaiting those who do not get on board. Though these fear-based strategies may result in short-term spurts of performance, people are incredibly clever in their ability to sabotage our efforts to rule by force.

It's going to be very difficult to bring a stop to this vicious circle of negatively reinforcing behaviors. It's like two gun fighters facing off for the draw. As soon as someone pulls a gun, the shooting begins.

Unfortunately, I think those of us who are organizationally empowered are the ones who must risk laying down our weapons first. In relationships where there is a longstanding history of one group having more power than the other, it's very unlikely that the oppressed parties will make themselves vulnerable first. Besides, it's quite a gift when we give someone our vulnerability! This gesture can set off a wonderful chain of events.

What's possible if we lay down our arms and turn to more peaceable means of getting things done? What can we do to create a workplace that feels nourishing and encouraging to the spirit? How can we convince people that it is safe for them to imagine that we really believe in them? How can we "lift the lid" and let people reach their heights?

I find that it takes courage to shift from providing warnings to offering unconditional support. Looking vigorously for opportunities to recognize accomplishments rather than jumping on errors and mistakes has taken considerable practice. Finding chances to say "You can do it" versus "You must do it" has not come easy.

I have heard that in order for "negative" feedback to have the desired results, I must give four times as much positive feedback as negative. This improves the chances that the person receiving the feedback will be more likely to accept the information and make a serious effort to change.

Imagine. We must give four times as much positive feedback as negative in order to create a nourishing atmosphere that encourages people to be the best that they can be. Wow! When I think about my various relationships at work and at home, I'm afraid my "nurturing ratio" is very deficient.

In discussing this concept with others, I've met with some skepticism. Some rejected the concept by claiming, "These are adults and they'll have to be tougher and more thick-skinned, if they're going to work with me." Others simply say, "I'm not a very complimentary kind of person. I'm not even that way with my spouse. They'll have to learn to live without praise from me."

Perhaps we can't expect the more reserved among us to have a personality transplant and become effusive with praise. However, I think that small positive changes can be accomplished without a lot of fanfare. Actually, I've found it doesn't seem to take much: a nod, a thank you, or a "nice job" note on the memo the employee wrote.

I wouldn't want to have to defend the validity of the "four times" praise theory. There is, however, an important and compelling message behind the theory. My fundamental discovery is that I must take steps to increase my actions that show respect and approval. If for no other reason, there seems to be fairly strong evidence that such changes in my behavior are required if I'm to get the support I need from others to accomplish the challenges I'm undertaking. Yet, I'm convinced that we can't sustain these changes in behavior unless we are driven by a greater sense of purpose than accomplishing performance goals. There will be too many times when expedient, short-term interests will cause us to retreat to old autocratic tactics.

To steady the course for the long haul, we must believe that people (including ourselves) deserve a more nourishing place to live and work. We must decide that creating a nourishing and supportive community is as important a goal as ensuring the longer term financial viability of our institutions. I don't believe that these goals are mutually exclusive. Quite the contrary. However, unless I keep them both in my sights at all times, I'm not able to hang in there when my early attempts to change the culture are met with skepticism, resistance, and disappointing results.

It's taken time. But when I persist, at some point, people

begin to trust my intentions, and I begin to trust theirs. It is then that the vicious circle of alienation becomes a virtuous circle of mutual trust and approval.

CHAPTER NINE

THE ADDICTIONS THAT DRIVE US

Many of us struggle with a "drug of choice." It may be alcohol, work, sex, eating, buying, or exercise, to name a few. In some cases, we are actually proud of our addictions, cleverly explaining the virtues of our excesses. And, indeed, some of our addictions are more virtuous than others.

Our explanations include working hard to give our family all that they deserve. Or, as we hobble back from our twenty-mile weekend run in preparation for our next marathon, we explain that we are doing it all for our continued good health. Alternatively, we assure friends or family members that the couple of glasses of wine we have each evening are a wise and appropriate way to relax and reduce stress.

It's difficult to know when these behaviors move from healthy to unhealthy roles in our lives, although there are some warning signals. For example, we may have worked long and hard for years, until we come to a point where we recognize that we really don't need more income to live comfortably. But we are still driven to work far more than is required by anyone other than ourselves. This may be a warning signal that we have become a workaholic.

If we have been experiencing running-related injuries, yet avoid going to a doctor because the thought of life without running terrifies us, it may be a warning.

If we continue to have affairs, even though we have a loving and satisfying relationship, it may be worth examining the role that addictive sex is playing in supporting our self-esteem.

We might be concerned if we keep making promises to ourselves that we consistently break. For example, if we keep saying to ourselves, I'm going to start working less, but it never happens, we may have a problem.

If we often go to bed at night saying to ourselves, I've been drinking too much lately, so I'm not going to drink tomorrow. Then we drink again anyway. We may need to come to grips with how powerless we are over our addiction.

Finally, in all of these matters relating to our excesses, we must listen very carefully to those concerns brought to our attention by significant people in our lives. We are vulnerable to blind spots in these matters. Because we can so easily become dependent on addictions and are reluctant to consider life without them, we would be wise to seek second and third opinions if someone has been concerned enough to give us a warning.

The problem with all of these addictions is that they

provide us with a convenient escape from "real life." They stunt our emotional growth. When the going gets tough emotionally, we return to our virtuous addictions and avoid dealing with life's complications and pains. Worse yet, we may be so deeply immersed that we don't even see that there are important emotional events going on around us that deserve our attention. We can be oblivious to the cries for help that we are getting from people because we have disappeared to be with our drug of choice.

Facing my addictions has been a real gift. It has reshaped my life and my relationships with all those around me. Unfortunately, like others, I didn't face up to my addictions until I encountered some serious problems. (Divorce, health problems, a child who gets into trouble, job loss, or mid-life crises are the more common forms of dramatic wake-up calls.) It's a pity that we require such drastic knocks on the head to get our attention.

It's sometimes more difficult for successful people to accept that we are in trouble with our addictions. Our image of addicts is destitute drunks who have lost their jobs and are living in cardboard shacks—people who have lost all control over their lives and who are powerless in the face of their addiction.

But the only difference is that some of us are more able to sustain an image of being in control than the street drunk.

We usually believe we are better people or have stronger characters because the effects of our addictions seem less obvious and more socially acceptable.

In my own attempts to recover from various addictions, I have been amused at how I've used my "controlling craziness" to try to assist me in my recovery. Basically, I tried to overpower and control the addictions. So, stopping my drinking was relatively easy. However, because I'm much better at abstinence than moderation, dealing with my addiction to work has been much more difficult.

When we try to overcome our addictions by turning the full controlling power of our compulsive obsessiveness back on the addiction, we are in for trouble in the long run. We may successfully wrestle one addiction after another to the mat. However, our efforts can be like the proverbial ill-fated attempts to stick fingers in a dike that has hundreds of holes.

A friend of mine stopped drinking "cold turkey" over a decade ago. Since then he has waged continuous war on a wide range of other addictions. Though he has been single-handedly and proudly winning many of the battles, he has been exhausted for years. He has never really accepted his powerlessness over his addictions and, as a result, he's never reached out for help with the root cause of his struggles.

When we try to recover this way, we are called "dry drunks." This label applies equally well to those of us who use the same strategy for recovery from addictions other than alcohol.

If we wish to permanently escape from the cruel demons that capture our souls and drive us toward exhaustion, emotional destruction, and alienation from others, we must admit that because of our addictions our lives have become unmanageable. "Unmanageable" does not mean "failure" or "unsuccessful." It simply means that our addictions are running our lives. Obviously, this admission is a monstrous step, but it's only in our admission of powerlessness that we regain our power. As long as we are trying to "control" our addictions, it will continue to feel as though we have a mad dog on a leash that is likely to get away from us at any moment. The energy that we put into trying to restrain the mad dog is exhausting. Little energy is left to examine whose dog it is and why it's along for the journey.

As I have attempted to get to know this mad dog, rather than simply restrain him, I have been on a difficult spiritual and emotional journey. I have needed help with this journey from family, friends, therapists, spiritual guides, support groups, and twelve-step programs.

Investing in this emotional and spiritual journey has had great payoff for me. It's a shame that we sometimes invest more in our educational or physical growth and wellness than in our emotional and spiritual wellness. For me, there has been more leverage for personal and professional success in the latter than in the former.

As my commitment to understanding my addictions has grown, many joys and successes have followed. I've begun to feel that I am running my own life. I've stopped feeling as though I am being controlled by some dark, unmanageable inner madness. My addictions continue to cause me pain from time to time, but they have lost the power to control me.

The energy that I formerly wasted on controlling myself can be rechanneled now toward creative and regenerative pursuits. I feel liberated to do my job and lead my life more fully.

Freed of these "heads-down, damn-the-torpedoes, full-speed-ahead" addictions, I am more available for real contact with everyone and less likely to miss opportunities to give and get support.

There is a great sense of joy and peace that has come from letting the mad dog go.

CHAPTER TEN

ON BEING ENLIGHTENED
BUT NOT EVOLVED

The pressure is mounting for major changes in how we manage and relate to the world around us. People in all aspects of our lives are demanding greater power and participation in matters affecting their lives. Nobody wants to be told to do anything anymore.

These shifting power dynamics are calling for dramatic new ways of engaging with others at work and outside of work. The demand for change is heightened by the fact that life has become so complicated. Most of us are beginning to understand that we require the support and involvement of many diverse partners to deal with life's challenges. Little of significance can be accomplished by oneself these days. Perhaps it was always that way, but it used to feel easier to "go it alone."

I don't believe that the new ways of responding to these changing demands and requirements have been invented yet. We are all experimenting. Actually, it feels more like muddling than experimenting. This can be very disconcerting. Particularly when many "experts" around us seem to be so clear about what we should be doing.

Several months ago I was having breakfast with three other management consultants who were discussing their experiences and frustrations with their clients. As the conversation proceeded, they were all criticizing their clients for not getting on board with the new ways of participative management. As the conversation went on, I became increasingly uncomfortable. My consultant friends were very clear about how these new ways of managing were to be practiced; but in the course of running my own twenty-five-person company, I was constantly uncertain about what was required of me as a participative leader/manager.

In reflecting on my colleagues' conversation and my reaction to it, I was reminded of the particular difficulty we all have in negotiating the unclear passage from the old ways to the new ways. We are very clear about the need for change, but we also recognize the high risks involved in moving from a controlling to a more participative culture. We have a strong desire to be perfect; yet, the rules for being perfect haven't been invented. Then, there are consultants and others talking to us as though they really understand what we should be doing; they imply that if we were of the right spirit or right mind, we'd abandon our old ways immediately.

These ambiguous and threatening conditions and shaming accusations—from within and without—can have a very negative impact on our openness to change. They can cause us to become even more controlling and rigid, at a time that requires us to be flexible and loose. As a result, we must be respectful and generous to ourselves during this change process. We must also require that those who would support us do so with great respect and care for our legitimate resistances and doubts about where this is all leading. For if we allow ourselves to be shamed or pushed prematurely (by ourselves or others) into a new way of being, we run the risk that our immune systems will resist the change entirely. We will become unable or unwilling to move forward with the required spirit of creativity and experimentation. On the other hand, we can't delay in our journey to get aligned with these new realities.

Faced with the enormous risks and dichotomies associated with moving from the old ways to the new ways, we can reasonably predict certain stages of behavior in ourselves and others. Though these stages can be characterized as normal, we must take special care to stay alert to the unique challenges that we face in passing from one to the other.

The four stages are persistence, resistance, co-option, and renewal.

In the first stage, we persist in old behaviors. This stage is often characterized by an outright denial that any change is required and a redoubling of our efforts, using tried and true methods. When these efforts don't produce the desired results, we conclude that the problem lies with a deficiency of execution by ourselves or others, and we try again, harder—back to the basics!

The second stage, the resistance stage, is often hard to recognize as progress, by either ourselves or others. In this stage we become argumentative and angry, yearning for the old days. We begin to recognize that things are in fact changing and that many of our old responses are inadequate; it makes us damned mad and frustrated. Our behavior may scare us and others, but it is important to remember that this is progress. Until we start to resist, we haven't begun to recognize that any change is required.

The third stage, co-option, brings unique challenges for us and those around us. In this stage, we talk a good game, but we haven't really internalized the changes. We are enlightened but not evolved. We talk about things like empowerment, appreciation of diversity, and so on; but we can't really sustain a constant and reliable pattern of behavior, at home or in the workplace. During this stage we make ourselves and others quite crazy. Our behavior is somewhat schizophrenic. We can wax eloquent on most modern, politically-correct topics, but the lives we lead do not align with our rhetoric.

This third stage is where many organizations and

recovering autocrats find themselves in the early nineties. It is hoped that we are at this point because of our genuine recognition of a need for significant personal and organizational change. However, since many of us have such a strong need for approval, we may be content to just talk a good game and bask in the considerable affirmation that we can get by expressing ourselves on such important topics with such sensitivity. We can become content to stay enlightened but not evolved. As a further complication, we may honestly believe that we are "walking our talk"; we may be blind to the inconsistencies in our behavior. This is a particularly frustrating and dangerous time in our evolution, for us and others.

Before we can move to stage four, renewal, we must conduct a fearless inventory of where we really stand. A personal example of the hazards and delusions that are characteristic of this stage may be helpful.

In the past I found myself frequently proclaiming the virtues of creating an empowered work force, while also aware that there were many decisions I was making without meaningful involvement and input from others. I hadn't really bought into "participation," let alone "empowerment," which is much further along the participation continuum. My behavior of extolling a commitment to empowerment prior to mastering some reasonable levels of participation created a level of cognitive and emotional dissonance that disrupted my evolution.

I remain guilty of many examples of stage three, co-optive, behavior as I try to move from enlightened to evolved. My rhetoric is often unsubstantiated by my behavior. This is not in itself a problem. As a matter of fact, it's a necessary step in our evolution. It *is* a problem if we don't keep going. If we allow ourselves to be satisfied with an intellectual understanding of the issue and avoid the deeper, personal development that is required to affect real change and renewal, however, we can do little more than maintain a respectable veneer. Enough perhaps to sustain us in some situations, but not enough if we are committed to real change!

In the end, the idea is not to become superficially adjusted (enlightened). Rather, it will be necessary for us to do the personal work that is required to be profoundly corrected (evolved) in our hearts.

CHAPTER ELEVEN

USING THE GIFT OF POWER

Most people who have power (particularly positional power) have become the brunt of very serious criticism in recent times. Often, they are despised and held accountable for many of the problems at home, in our places of business, and in the country at large.

As a white male, I have been particularly sensitive to the rising distrust and anger directed at all those in power. Though white men don't have a corner on the power market, we do have a substantial market share. And we don't have to look far to discover abuses of power with which we can be associated.

Last year I was invited, along with ten other people, to meet weekly to review and comment on some research and writings on power by a friend of mine. The meetings were lively, animated, and thought provoking. Inevitably, most conversations turned to disturbing personal accounts of the misuse of power.

These conversations, though informative, were very painful for me to hear because they were often reporting experiences with people just like me: people in positions of

power. Though there was no denying the validity or seriousness of the stories, I found myself frequently uneasy with the
negative generalizations about those of us in power. It felt as
though my colleagues didn't have the full picture. Because few
of the participants in the group had ever held an executive
position in an organization, it was tempting for me to conclude
that they just couldn't be counted on to have a balanced view
of the uses and misuses of power.

In the weeks that followed, there was a great deal of discussion that called for the abandonment of the warriorlike
behaviors traditionally associated with the use of power. Other
discussions heralded the contributions that amplifying our
feminine side could have in eliminating these power struggles.

Again, though I saw the wisdom in all of these strategies,
I still found myself feeling uneasy with the implication that I
should throw away my sword and walk on the soft side. In
retrospect, I'm not certain that the group was suggesting this.
It is significant, however, that when people start talking about
abuses of power, recovering autocrats like me are not able to
hear them without becoming defensive and imagining that
they ultimately want us to become impotent and powerless.

A number of people in the research group did see all uses
of power as bad. As a result, the dynamics that were set up in
the group were not unlike those that exist in the world at large.
Those of us in power either deny or are defensive about our

abuses of power, while those who see themselves as not in power are relentless in their conviction that all power corrupts and all in power are corrupt.

I'm sad to report that the group dissolved after four or five meetings. I have speculated that the demise was a metaphor for the dilemmas that we all face in coming to terms with the power of power in our personal and organizational lives. Inevitably, if we take a deep look at it, in ourselves and others, it is quite frightening. We're afraid to have it and we're afraid not to have it. We may admire the good use of it by others, but we're terrified at the possibility that it could be turned against us.

Occasionally, as in my research group, we have an intellectually interesting exploration of the topic. Sometimes we butt heads over the issues, perhaps in response to a particularly disturbing example of an abuse of power. In the end, however, the opposing camps often return to their lives even more rigidified in their beliefs about power.

We who are in power continue to assume that we are entitled to have it and that we do not misuse it. Those who do not have power do not expect to get it; they don't want it and they don't trust anyone with it. To their credit and as evidence of their consistency, they don't even trust themselves with it.

This deadlock between the "haves" and "have-nots" is disempowering and de-motivating for all of us. The resentful have-nots can be exceptional in their ability to sabotage the efforts of those in power. Those of us who are in power, faced with the frustrating effects of sabotage or resistance to our use of power, can draw our warrior's swords and cut destructive paths across our organizations.

It would be useful for both sides to view power much like the wind. First of all, it exists. Even if all we can see is its effects, there is no denying it. When we catch it skillfully in our sails, we can use it to navigate the world. But it's unwise to deny the potential for destruction in its unbridled fury.

Like the wind, power should be cherished and respected. We all have responsibility for taking full advantage of this wonderful source of energy. Those who have the most power have a special responsibility for leading the way in terms of learning, experimentation, and self-management regarding its use. We must recognize and be thankful for the gift that we have been given. Some of us were given the gift as a birthright. Again, although being a white male is no guarantee of access to power, very often not being a white male has considerably limited access.

It is tempting for me to feel shameful about having power—particularly when I accept the part of my power that is a pure gift and has come to me as part of the package associated with my race, gender, and family of origin. Then, when I take a serious look at my past and present uses and abuses of power, that vision can add additional fuel to the fire.

It has been helpful to me to differentiate between guilt and shame. Guilt is the legitimate remorse I feel when I understand that I have wronged or harmed others. Shame, on the other hand, is a feeling of personal unworthiness and self-degradation. By these definitions it has felt appropriate for me to experience an occasional pang of guilt as I get an ever-more accurate picture of my uses of power. Nevertheless, I haven't found it helpful to engage in self-flagellation regarding abuses of power. Rather, supported by the insights that come from paying more attention to my uses and abuses of power, I'm beginning to trust myself more with power. I'm free to energetically look for worthy ways to use and share it.

While I'm enjoying the gift of power and looking for more respectful and worthy ways to use and share it, I still find it necessary to stay alert to my potential for returning to my more autocratic ways—that is, a sense of entitlement, hoarding, and a denial of my misuses.

To stay centered and "right-minded," I find it useful to regularly do an audit of whether it feels like I'm spending a lot of time grasping for power in my life—or am I spending more time enjoying the privilege of sharing it and using it wisely? This simple check has become a useful barometer to guide my journey.

CHAPTER TWELVE

PUTTING PEOPLE TO THE TEST

Fifteen years ago I worked for a very dynamic CEO who took great pride in putting people to the test. He didn't like job descriptions. He didn't see much need for organization charts. And he particularly disliked getting people together for team building or role clarification discussions. His basic approach was to "throw people in a pit and see who crawls out." His point of view was that you should hire the best people, and then just get out of their way. "The cream will rise to the top."

Though I had great affinity with his distaste for unnecessary bureaucratic processes, there was something quite soulless in his methods. There were many casualties in the pit and a lot of drownings in the cream. Yet, in the autocratic, imperialistic, competitive culture that prevailed, few if any of us saw his methods as anything but a noble test of our talent and tenacity.

Schooled over the past several decades in various versions of such survival-of-the-fittest techniques and having passed the tests ourselves, many of us have included some form of these noble testing processes in the way we manage today. As a matter of fact, the tougher things get, the more we are inclined to turn to these sink-or-swim tactics.

The culture that evolves from these methods promotes the idea that "the best are perfect," and we'll just replace the rest. Though there is much to recommend a relentless dedication to acquiring top talent and then giving them an opportunity to demonstrate superior performance, there are lots of flaws inherent in a single-minded use of this approach.

One such flaw is that there is not a limitless pool of perfect candidates to draw upon. And, with the accelerating competition for the best, the price of acquisition will be ever higher and the available talent increasingly more limited. Further, even the best are having trouble sustaining their image as "perfect," given the incredible knowledge explosion and the concomitant need for accelerated learning and continuous improvement.

It's likely that we will have more and more occasions where nobody appears to measure up to the tasks at hand. Then, we will be required to figure out how we can develop and encourage everyone's performance! Our old pit bull tactics will simply not produce the widespread levels of competence that will be required to compete in today's world. The old idea will not hold that a few of the best people, who have passed the test, can do all of the thinking, while other survivors of the competition will crawl up from the pit to enthusiastically follow them.

Shifting from a testing to a developmental mentality will not come easy. It will require a fundamental shift of the mind. Maybe even a shift of soul.

Five years ago I had an experience that dramatically illustrated the extent of the mind shift that I would personally have to undergo. I was consulting for two weeks with eighteen executives, each from a different country. They all worked for a very large, multi-national, United States-based company, and each was responsible for Human Resource Development in his particular country. The purpose of our time together was to share insights into the similarities and differences that we faced in ensuring that the company was developing the talent necessary to meet future requirements.

Several times during the first week I was fascinated with the stories told by the representative from Japan. Like many others, I had heard the legends that were developing about the use of teams in Japan. And, I must confess, I had a great deal of suspicion that the legends could not measure up to the realities. So I decided to invite my Japanese colleague to dinner one evening to see if I could "test" his legends. If the truth be known, I think I was hoping to find convincing evidence of the cross-cultural incompatibility of his approaches.

During dinner I got right to the point by asking a question that had been plaguing me all week: "If one of your team members isn't pulling his share of the load, what do the others do?"

Without batting an eye, he replied, "We help him."

Undeterred, I followed quickly with my second question: "What if he still doesn't do his part, after you've helped him?"

Again, with no hesitation, my dinner guest said, "We help him some more."

Now, I was getting frustrated. I wanted to know when they would decide that the team member had failed the test. So I jumped to my bottom-line question: "What if, in the end, the team member just can't carry his full load?"

With no apparent recognition of my mounting frustration, he responded, "We continue to work together to help get the job done."

As the conversation went on it became clear to me that my Japanese colleague and I were not able to communicate very easily on this issue. We were speaking a different language. We were operating from a different paradigm. In essence, I wanted to know how long the performance test would go on before they would fire or redeploy the person. My associate and his team members back in Japan, on the other hand, were apparently unwilling to frame the situation as a test.

As a person who had been taught for years to base my reputation on my ability to pick the winners and take decisive action when people did not measure up, I regarded this way of thinking as a major threat. I had always taken pride in the fact that I had demonstrated great courage in getting rid of the losers. No matter how difficult the circumstances, I never let relationships cloud my judgment when it came to evaluating performance and taking the appropriate action. Even if the person had become a friend, I was willing to act. And I didn't have much respect for those who were unwilling to follow my tough-minded example.

Not only did I view this as almost a moral issue, I also saw it as a primary weapon in my arsenal of management practices for ensuring accountability and high performance.

Now, I'm not prepared to make a case for the total cross-cultural transferability of the concepts practiced by some Japanese teams. There are complicated dynamics that muddy the waters on this issue. For example, there are significant differences related to individualism versus collectivism that are at play between the two cultures. I've come to believe, however, that there are important messages to be learned from these contrasting paradigms. We must look more at where the finger is pointing than at the details of how our Japanese friends act on their beliefs. If we look at the details of their methods, it will be easy to find innumerable reasons why a more developmental versus a performance approach won't work here. On the other hand, if we look at the spirit behind their actions, there is much to be learned.

At the most fundamental level, our biggest gains will come from shifting substantially more emphasis to the core concepts of continuous development and support instead of continuous testing. It is questionable whether our old survival-of-the-fittest techniques ever served us well. However, it is unquestionable that they are a great liability at this point in history.

We cannot afford at this time to have people who are afraid to take risks. A "testing culture" creates a level of fear that discourages legitimate and necessary risk taking. At a time when we need people to set stretch goals and reach for the stars to gain competitive advantage, we can't be standing by with our "pass/fail" report cards in hand.

Innovation will not flourish where mistakes are perceived to be career threatening. Teamwork and collaboration are in serious jeopardy when all concerned feel as though they are competing for a limited number of prizes—and the rules are: "May the best person win!"

People cannot sustain long-term performance and commitment when they feel as though they are always on the line with us. The stress is unbearable when they are made to feel as though every project, every meeting, every conflict is a test of their essential worth and value: Prove yourself. Don't fail. Don't make a mistake!

Innovation, risk taking, creativity, and performance are

among the rewards for creating a climate where people come to work each day to express themselves—not to prove themselves! In addition, all of our souls begin to heal when we acknowledge that our essence and real value originate in the universe, not in some "noble test" that we have created for us and others to pass here in our corporations.

CHAPTER THIRTEEN

INFORMATION AS AN ALLY

There is great power in information. Many careers have been built on an ability to access and manage information. It can be a great source of control; therefore, we who have it are cautious about sharing it. We dole it out on a "need to know" basis.

But this retentive and fearful approach to information management is becoming difficult to sustain even for the most controlling individuals. Technology is making information widely available in organizations. The complexities of the modern business environment demand that everyone be more self-managing and capable of making complex, on-the-spot decisions. And this capability is dependent on broad-based information availability. Continued use of antiquated management practices will not serve us well as we try to overcome our fears and get on board with the undeniable need to more widely distribute information.

Two of the more common ways that information is used include 1) making certain that we and our organizations are viewed in the best possible light at all times, and 2) identifying where expectations are not being met by others so that we can take corrective action.

Though a good case can be made for the positive use of information in both situations, my past practices have sometimes been excessive and dysfunctional. In the first case, I used information predominantly for self-promotion or damage control. "Family secrets" were carefully protected. If something wasn't going as planned, I kept it to myself. Only the inner circle had access to potentially damaging data that could be misunderstood. I did not take kindly to suggestions that information be more widely distributed.

In the second case, the information I had regarding the performance gaps of others was often used unwisely. I used it as a sword, not as a lamp to help shed light on topics. Ironically, this confirmed everyone's fear about information getting into the wrong hands.

In the years that I worked as a senior executive at several large companies, an interesting and common characteristic became apparent. Many of us spent a great deal of time developing strategies and tactics to gain competitive advantage in the marketplace. Then, once we agreed on these strategies to ensure customer focus, quality, productivity, just-in-time inventory, and the like, we *allegedly* began to gather information to track and report our progress toward achieving these goals.

Allegedly! More often we spent our time trying to use the information to prove to one another that we were well on our way to achieving our goals. Our monthly status reports to the boss, quarterly reports to the Board, and updates at our team meetings painted very favorable pictures of our accomplishments and, cleverly, rationalized or deflected attention from things that would reflect less favorably on our performance. Our reports were not usually outright lies; rather, they were obfuscations, denials, and avoidances that had an insidious longer-term effect on our perception of reality. It was our belief that an honest reporting of the facts was not in our best interests. And, besides, that's not the way the game was being played by our colleagues.

To further complicate matters, there seemed to be a rule that nobody would be indiscreet enough to point out that someone else wasn't reporting progress accurately. If someone violated the rule, we usually counterattacked. If the behavior persisted, we stopped having team meetings and worked one-on-one with the boss.

We did not feel safe sharing the real facts with our colleagues because information did not feel like an ally. We saw it as a threat. We did not trust ourselves and others to respectfully work together to use the information to do collaborative problem solving. We believed that others would not understand our situation or would use the information against us.

This charade was costly—from an emotional and a performance standpoint. For it is only in fully understanding the gap between where we are and where we want to be that we can mobilize and create energy for real change. We build and grow based on reality, not fiction. Since we didn't have good information about performance gaps, we were at great risk. Our sanitized reporting resulted in a denial of "what is," while we created a sense of well-being that was stultifying. Hours, days, and months of "corporate-speak" communications delayed us from getting down to working on things that we all knew we had been denying or avoiding. Sometimes we even began to believe our own misleading status reports, and then we were *really* headed for trouble.

At the root of these fears and destructive practices is an old nemesis: the belief that we must be perfect if we are to retain the respect and admiration of those around us. Or, worse yet, we believe that we actually are perfect. We feel as though we are either heroes or failures. There is no in-between. Any suggestion that we are less than perfect is quite painful. Less-than-glowing information about our performance, no matter how well-intended or presented, feels like criticism.

When I am given negative feedback, at work or at home, I'm still shocked at how I overreact at times. Even though I may be effective at not letting anyone know how deeply the feedback affects me, I'm often shaken and upset. My only conclusion about my consistent overreaction is that I have not yet fully come to terms with the fact of my imperfection.

Coincidentally, since I feel such a personal compulsion to be perfect, sometimes I project the same demand for perfection onto others. I put myself and them on pedestals, only to be disappointed that we can't stay there in the face of information to the contrary. I shift between a sense of false pride and a sense of loathing myself and others.

Here is the root cause of my fear of information: since obviously I am not perfect, it is predictable that any accurate information about my performance will by definition dispense with the myth of my perfection.

It seems to me that a solution to this dilemma lies in recognition of the fact that our collective success is inextricably connected to our ability to create a vision for the future and then to determine honestly, on a continual basis, how we are falling short of our vision. To do that we must develop a greatly enhanced appetite and tolerance for honest self-assessment and feedback. We must see information as an ally, not an enemy.

There is nothing wrong with thinking less of myself and others when we fall short of our best efforts. However, these assessments must be no more nor less than the truth. More information and less drama are called for. Fits of aggrandizement or loathing will only be an obstacle to establishing a climate that builds trust and encourages open and honest communication.

To achieve this climate where information is seen as an ally rather than an enemy, I have discovered that I must be immeasurably kinder to myself and others. I must relieve myself and others of the well-intentioned but neurotic desire to be seen as perfect. This is easier when I avoid the frightening giant swings from hero to heel. A steady, ongoing, and sober look at reality is needed to produce a culture that is committed to using information to create the future, not denounce the past.

Our key resource in the nineties isn't capital or even people but knowledge and information. If we can create a culture that sees information as an ally and then uses it very respectfully, we will be able to substantially leverage this vital asset.

CHAPTER FOURTEEN

THE TAO OF HOMOGENEITY

Homogeneity is one of the more reliable ways to ensure control. People of the same race, gender, education level, and economic status are more likely to hold similar opinions and views than those who differ in these characteristics. It's not a sure thing that they will agree, but for the purpose of enhancing our ability to predict and manage outcomes, it's often a good bet. Pollsters and marketing gurus have capitalized on this hypothesis for decades.

Since we take such pleasure in being able to control our destiny, being in a homogeneous environment can be very comforting. The fact that historically we have found ourselves surrounded by people just like ourselves may be accidental or planned, intended or unintended. Nevertheless, as the world around us becomes more and more diverse, if we are honest, we will admit to the emotional and lifestyle obstacles that interfere with our full welcoming of diversity. We're not entirely certain what's in it for us to do so.

On the emotional side, we take comfort from having

people around us who can be counted on to share similar viewpoints. This makes our lives feel less threatening and more manageable.

As to lifestyle, many of us lead lives that result in major isolation from people who are substantially different from us. Over the years, I have found myself cloistered in offices, neighborhoods, churches, and social circles that have offered limited opportunities to have meaningful contact with a wide range of human beings. In that milieu, my political, social, and economic viewpoints seldom came under serious attack or challenge by my associates.

Sometimes, driven by values or guilt, I made attempts to broaden my associations and to connect my life more meaningfully to a wider representation of the human family. Unfortunately, these well-meaning efforts were often rather distant, sporadic, and clumsy. Hiring an African-American manager, making a donation to a worthy cause, promoting a woman as a manager, or collecting food for the church's food basket were well-intentioned but essentially sanitized ways to get my hands on the soul of life. In the absence of significant experiences with people different from me, my connections were often paternalistic and distant.

I once worked for a CEO who was very active in a wide range of worthy community affairs. He regularly encouraged his managers to do their part in achieving the company's affirmative-action goals. However, after one college recruiting season when I had been particularly successful in hiring women and people of color for our training program, he called me to his office and said, "I'm glad you're making progress in supporting our affirmative-action goals, but you better make damned certain that you hire enough white males to help me run this place in the future!" I fear that we are all capable of variations on this theme—unless we can find some way to escape the restrictive boundaries of our normal lives and find our essential connection with the whole of humankind.

I have discovered that there are enormous joys, blessings, and commercial payoffs in connecting with the magnificent variety of human experience that is available to me. Granted, at times I have to sacrifice some predictability and comfort—and that can be frightening. But the old adage, "variety is the spice of life," cannot be realized without some measure of experimentation and risk taking.

Several years ago I was working with a team of consultants who were designing a one-week executive development program for the top executives of a large financial services organization. One of the objectives for the program was to have the senior management team explore their personal values and relate them to the issues they faced together in running their company. The group was comprised of fifteen white men and one white woman.

It was unlikely that this fairly homogeneous group would produce a rich and varied debate about values. One of our curriculum design team members came up with an incredibly creative solution that the company accepted. For the two days while we addressed the issue of values, we invited as full participants in the debates a 50-year-old white, male, eighteen-wheel truck driver; a mid-30s female prison warden; a 40ish former housewife who had just completed her undergraduate degree; and a young African-American actor.

Prior to the session, all of the participants were given a wide range of materials to read. The materials ranged from Plato to selections from the Bible, a newly-written experimental play, and excerpts from current news magazines. A skilled process facilitator led the group through lively Socratic explorations of the values and beliefs that were woven throughout these readings. Particular emphasis was placed on getting people to discuss how they differed and why they felt the way they did, as well as the implications of their beliefs for how they lead their lives.

The results were dramatic! Some participants reported significant changes in long-held personal beliefs. Others stuck strongly to most of what they believed before they came to the session, but expressed marvelous new levels of understanding regarding diverse viewpoints. All felt deeply moved by the experience of getting to know and respect the opinions and life experiences of people whom they would not encounter during the normal course of their lives.

As an observer of the process, I was equally deeply affected by the events of the two days. First of all, I was touched and encouraged by the level of intimacy that developed between the participants. It gave me great hope for humanity, demonstrating what can be achieved if we can just find ways to spend more meaningful time together.

Another emotion that engulfed me was jealousy: I wanted desperately to be a participant in the discussions. Though getting a chance to watch the process was a rare privilege, nothing could replace actually being part of the discussions.

The irony of my jealousy became clear as the two days went on. Wouldn't it be wonderful if I could transfer this desire to be part of these debates to my daily life? What if I suddenly began to feel deprived, left out, and limited if I didn't regularly have a wide range of people in my life? What if I began to yearn for more diversity anytime I spent too many days in a row with "my own kind"?

Part of the American conscience since our founding has been the dream of equality. It is rooted in our religious heritage and woven into our Constitution; its banner has been carried by such distinguished advocates as Martin Luther King. It has never been fully realized, however. My guess is that we will never make breakthroughs toward this dream as long as so many of us spend most of our time in homogeneous clusters, deprived of the opportunities to peer into each other's souls.

As a recovering autocrat I am facing many challenges to engage more equally with everyone with whom I interact. I have learned techniques and management practices that promote equality, but it's hard to imagine that I can legitimately sustain a more egalitarian style until I begin to feel more connected and equal to those around me. And I believe that this is only possible if I can make certain that I am not isolated in a homogeneous cocoon.

Everyone probably does not have an equal ability to contribute in the workplace. And not everyone is equally suited to become close friends. But as my life includes more diversity, I begin to recognize that we all have an equal right to respect, an equal right to access opportunity, an equal right to participate in matters affecting our lives, an equal right to expect genuine care and concern from each other, and an equal right to be treated in a way that is neither paternalistic nor condescending.

My past sense of comfort and control may have come from isolation. My new sense of comfort and joy is coming from diverse human experiences that increase my realization that all people are equally capable of goodness and love—and equally deserving of my goodness and love.

CHAPTER FIFTEEN

ELIMINATING SOUL POLLUTION

Many businesses are hostile and unfriendly to the human spirit. "Rigid," "restrictive," and "punishing" are familiar words used by employees to describe the culture in which they work.

Dissatisfaction with organizational culture doesn't seem to be confined to hourly workers. Executives and managers are equally likely to express pain and concern about unhealthy climates in their companies. It's not unusual for employees to report feelings of victimization by some mysterious "they," who have defined the corporate rules by which the employees must live.

The "soul pollution" that exists in an organizational environment can have as significant of an impact on us as the pollution of our natural world. Sometimes those of us responsible for "climate control" in organizations deny that the problem is really serious. Or, we may recognize the seriousness but be unwilling to give up our right to "pollute." Why should we have to change our habits when those who preceded us did just as they pleased? Or, we may think that it's hopeless to believe that we can get enough people to commit to making real changes in their behavior.

The net effect of such responses can be lethal. No real attempt is made to clean up the environment. This can put our personal health and that of subsequent working generations at serious risk—as organizations choke the life out of human beings, including ourselves. And it isn't always easy to see how we can make a real difference.

Our families are another place where we can feel frustrated and wounded by dysfunctional social and emotional legacies. In my own case, I inherited many wonderful things from my family, but there are significant aspects of the inheritance that are unhealthy and cause great pain for me and others. These pollutants in the family environment have been passed on for years. By the time they got to my generation, they felt quite intractable, being embedded in the DNA of the family. These dysfunctional characteristics include such tendencies as alcoholism and "cutting-off," or disowning, family members who don't fit into an approved mold.

It's not easy to accept responsibility for cleaning up the environment, whether in the business world, the natural world, or the family. For a number of years I made some perfunctory gestures to do my part, gestures that were primarily driven by a sense of responsibility and a desire for approval.

So, at home, with my wife's encouragement, I began to make some modest efforts to recycle waste. At work, when employee attitude surveys revealed some concerns about the climate in our organization, I "responsibly" tried to take some actions to improve matters. And, when my grown children started to report the results of their therapy, I consented to look more deeply at some of the forces that had been governing our family relationships for decades.

There was not much passion in my early ventures into these cleanup efforts. I was dutiful, but, if the truth be known, I was also somewhat resentful. The destruction of the earth's atmosphere seemed quite remote to me. My position in my organization allowed me considerable personal protection from the hazards in our work climate. And, why couldn't my kids be content to "honor their mother and father," just as I had been taught to do?

Though there are gains to be made in the present from our efforts, it also became clearer to me that the significant gains will be reserved for future generations. Since a capacity for delayed gratification is not a common strength among people like myself (we are more inclined to be instant-gratification junkies), I had another explanation for my less than enthusiastic advances into the difficult, long-term efforts required for this cleanup work. As one of the privileged of this world, it's taken a long time for me to consider sacrificing my present entitlements and conveniences in service of a legacy.

My personal sources of inspiration and motivation for change have come from some unexpected quarters. First of all, I've passed the age of 50. Apparently, if you're lucky enough to get past 50, the Creator has automatically programmed you to think more deeply about leaving a legacy in which you can take pride. It seems that at this age we start to care more about what those who follow will think of our contributions to their world. Aging doesn't ensure that we'll be converted, nor do we have to be 50-plus to get on board. However, it's a big help!

Another source of inspiration came from the messages that Native Americans offer us on this topic. One such message is that the future is with us right now. Native Americans say, "The seventh generation is coming up out of the ground right behind us." For some reason, this message is very empowering and motivating to me. The idea that the beliefs and behaviors that I'm promulgating now can shape the lives of those who are seven generations beyond is quite stimulating. It gives me a sense that my efforts can live on and endure. Also, it gives much more meaning and depth to the Native American idea that "we are the grandfathers and grandmothers of tomorrow." It makes me feel as though the little things that I do today can make a big difference as they cascade into the future. Even if their benefit at the moment is hard to perceive.

The biggest breakthrough in my commitment to leaving

behind a better world came at the time of my mother's death. She had survived my father by five years, so her death marked the final passing of the family's "culture care" to me and my kids. Since I'm an only child, this responsibility weighed heavily on me during the three days immediately following her death.

At the funeral home and at other family events leading up to her burial, I was disturbed that there was so much unfinished business between my mother and her family members. Oh, there was certainly no absence of stories that were told about her, and many were humorous and entertaining. However, most of the stories were accompanied by spoken or unspoken memories of pain, anger, or disappointment about a level of intimacy that never existed between mother and anyone else in the family. As a result, there was a marked lack of intense grieving and pain. This is not to deny that there were many family issues that got stirred up by her death, but the sad fact was that there was little wailing at the loss of her personal presence in our lives. As a matter of fact, there was some relief at the prospect of not having to deal with her unpleasantness in the future.

I was devastated by these observations. Further, I was overcome with a desire to do my part to change the course of those family patterns that had brought us to this regrettable place. Before closing the casket and proceeding to the grave site, I asked my wife and kids to join me for a few private moments at my mother's side. I told them that with my mother's death, we were now the keepers of our family's future. I acknowledged that my parents had handed down some wonderful things to me, which I had tried to pass on to them. However, I had also received some "craziness" that regrettably I had made some unconscious attempts to pass their way, too.

I reported how painful it had been to see my mother's life come to an end with so much unresolved between her and the rest of us and so much lost intimacy, never to be regained. I said to them, "When I die and you are gathering to say your good-byes to me, I would like it to be much different. And, when you die, I hope that there will be an even greater level of intimacy between you and those that you leave behind. We have a real chance to let go of many of the legacies that my mother and father unfortunately could not cast aside in their lifetime. We can stop alcoholism in our family. We can make certain that no one ever gets disowned again. We can make a difference. The simple gestures that we make can be very healing for us and for generations to come. Let's dedicate the rest of the time that we have together to creating a family legacy of healing and intimacy."

My "speech" was clumsy, and the family seemed a little stunned at my unexpected remarks. Nevertheless, in the years that have followed, everyone seems to be operating at a different level of optimism, risk taking and caring as we deal with the difficult matters that every family faces. There appears to be a full-scale environmental cleanup under way in the family!

Perhaps it's easier to get enthused about trying to make our families healthier places in which to live than it is to get impassioned about our natural environment and the culture in our companies. Yet, I'm hopeful that the cost of ignoring the "pollution" in these areas (or perhaps the payoffs for dealing with it) will become increasingly obvious to all of us.

I'm reminded of a touching and impactful environmental commercial from the 1980s. The commercial showed an aging Native American with a tear in his eye. The tear had been brought on by his painful recognition of the devastation that was being heaped on our streams and air. This wise and caring man's pain was a wake-up call for all of us.

It is my hope that in the years to come we can all look with similar pain at any violation of any environments of which we are part. And that our efforts to clean up our natural world and our family and company environments will permeate all that we do—creating and leaving behind a better world for all.

CHAPTER SIXTEEN

TRAINED FOR SHOW

Many of us have been trained for show. We have been carefully taught how to dress, eat, and behave in all situations. In many ways, this training has been a real blessing. It has served us well in our pursuit of success and social acceptance. Those who have not had access to this training are at a serious competitive disadvantage in many life situations.

When I was 38 years old and had become a vice president at a prestigious bank, I invited my parents to have lunch with me in the executive dining room. This seemed like a fitting way to celebrate my promotion and good fortune. After I placed our order, my mother gazed proudly around the room and then turned to me and said, "It certainly is a good thing that your father and I taught you good manners or you never would have gotten to this place in life." I said, "Thank you, Mother. That's true." But I also remember feeling a twinge of unexplainable resentment—something like I used to feel as a teenager when my parents would insist that I play the clarinet for visiting friends.

Depending on the decade in which you were raised, your parents and other concerned teachers and mentors spent considerable energy keeping you from becoming a beatnik, hippy, or punk rocker. Perhaps you "trained easily," or you may have put up quite a struggle. In the end, like me, you have probably learned the rules. You know how to put on a good show. And you have found some way to deny, ignore, or resolve your version of the "angry kid" who didn't want to play the clarinet at your parents' beck and call.

Over the years I have had many confusing emotional reactions to the training that I received. Undoubtedly I have benefited immensely from this tutoring. Yet, I have often felt that I was giving up some very important parts of myself to be successful and accepted. I felt as though I was on a short leash that didn't give me much room to operate. And I wouldn't mind taking a bite out of the person who was holding the leash. Nevertheless, in most cases, I settled down and won "Best of Show" awards.

It's hard for those of us who have been properly trained and required to "show" not to pass on that training to our children and protégés. Actually, in the past, I've been shocked at how willing I've been to mindlessly pass on the words of wisdom that I was taught, without seriously challenging whether or not I really believed in what I was advocating. As a matter of fact, to my great surprise, I have often been as relentless as my parents were in insisting on proper dress, manners, and social conduct.

Certain of our organizational attempts to challenge or deviate from the rules of the show can be quite amusing. For example, many companies are having furious debates about the desirability of having dress-down days on Fridays. One large bank decided to permit casual dress on Fridays, but the company made buttons for all employees to wear that advised their customers not to worry, this was a special day at the bank! We'll be back to normal tomorrow.

If we enter the nineties having high levels of anxiety about issues like dress-down days, it's hard to imagine how we're going to truly unleash the creative human spirits in our organizations.

To complicate matters further, there are certain things that are required for success that can't be acquired by training. For example, I'm five foot six inches tall. My parents couldn't train the shortness out of me: like the proverbial swaybacked horse that wouldn't be considered for certain shows, because of my height, I'm automatically excluded from some competitions.

I've found it difficult to deal with the realities and resentments associated with demands to "be" or "behave" in certain ways when those standards have felt irrelevant as true measures of my effectiveness or worth. I have responded to the demands of my various trainers over the years in one of four ways: buckling down, marginalizing, bolting, or rationalizing.

When I have buckled down and played by others' rules for long periods of time, I've often begun to feel as though I were living someone else's life. And I have seriously wondered if I would ever get time to live my own life! As my fears about not reaching that desirable state mounted, my state of mind frequently led to bouts of hypochondria. Every little symptom became a subconscious reminder of my limited time on this earth. These fears of death and associated illnesses became a wake-up call to get back to (or find) my own life plan, not necessarily the one that I've been trained to follow.

Sometimes I've responded to the oppressive impact of others' expectations by marginalizing myself—that is, I would live up to most of the rules, but I'd do something counter-dependent that would marginally differentiate me from the other trainees. For example, when I first went into banking, I got rid of all of the sport coats I had acquired while working in retailing. (Blue pin-striped suits were nonnegotiable.) However, I kept various forms of facial hair as a small way of holding on to myself, or perhaps of thumbing my nose at the system. In the end, I didn't get away with anything. "The system" knew I really didn't accept its rules and found ways to exclude me.

One of my least effective ways of managing resentment over demands to conform has been to bolt, with no previous warning to those around me. This approach has been characterized by a sudden announcement of my intention to leave, only to have the other party (wife, boss, etc.) say, "I didn't know you were upset." This pattern of bolting is very familiar during mid-life crises.

My fourth method of responding has been to rationalize. In this mode, the full impact of my behaviors has come to bear on those around me. I totally embrace my parents' and mentors' rules and proceed to make certain that I'm as effective at "training" and getting compliance with the rules as they were. When I'm in this place, I'm not very open to challenges to the status quo. I take comfort in ignoring any information that might confuse me and cause me to revisit my own angst about lifelong compliance with rules of questionable relevancy to my own life.

In 1992 several articles appeared in newspapers across the nation about a young man who was leading a campus protest against the status quo by appearing naked at various university events. (This usually happens on campuses about once a decade.) At the time I speculated that he probably represents our collective worst fears of what happens when we don't accept the conventional wisdom of what's right and what's wrong. At some level, we all feel as though we're sitting on a primal, untrainable self who must be controlled or we'll get wild.

It's hard to deny that at an individual and organizational

level we do have a legitimate need for a semblance of social order. As we have discovered over and over again, however, we are in very dangerous territory when we are confronted with potentially uncontrollable parts of ourselves and others. Instead of getting to know, understand, respect, and even enjoy these parts, our response can be to become more rigid in our compliance, until we or someone else has to revolt in order to cast off the shackles that have been confining our spirits.

It's unlikely that most of us can become totally at peace with what we have to give up of ourselves to live in our modern business institutions. We will always be carrying some secrets in our hearts. However, if we can constantly pay attention to the parts of ourselves that don't want to "play the clarinet" on demand, perhaps we will be more responsive to our own needs and those of others. And we'll be more inclined to check our "lesson plans" before we begin training others.

CHAPTER SEVENTEEN

THE BIG WHEEL SYNDROME

Many of us are "big wheels" in the various forums in which we operate. In our companies, social networks, and families, we can be very naive about the impact we have on those around us. As "big wheels," we are connected to a long series of increasingly smaller wheels; thus, when we make minor revolutions, we cause the smaller wheels in the chain to rotate wildly.

I used to work with the CEO of a retail chain store who was famous for making visits to his many geographically dispersed stores. Though the store managers appreciated his attentions, the visits also made them quite nervous. To protect themselves from surprises, they secretly agreed to communicate with one another during the CEO's visits. As each visit was completed, the store manager would call the other stores scheduled for an inspection to pass on information about what the CEO was focusing on during this trip.

During one particular round of visits, the first store was severely criticized for poor standards of housekeeping. The demoralized store manager quickly called his colleagues and warned them to get ready for a "white glove" inspection. The six stores scheduled for visits in the next three days proceeded to pull out all the plugs to get everything spit-polished for the boss's arrival.

The remaining visits occurred without one mention of housekeeping. It turns out that the first store manager had a long history of poor housekeeping and the CEO had finally run out of patience with his performance. Since there was not a perceived housekeeping problem in the other stores, this item received no attention during the subsequent visits. However, it did receive considerable attention from the CEO when the next budget report was released. The six stores, overreacting to the warning of their colleague, had doubled their house-keeping expenses to solve a nonexistent problem!

This pattern of big-wheel action causing dramatic reactions is repeated time and again in organizations throughout the world. Such reactions (even if they are unintended) can have expensive consequences both in dollars and emotional chaos.

In addition to naive underestimations of our impact on others, there are other circumstances where we may be less innocent. In these cases, we can be blind to how our self-centeredness and sense of entitlement to others' attentions can cause harm.

A bank chairman, with whom I was consulting, recounted a sad tale of how his self-interests set off a chain of events that had very undesirable consequences. Late one Friday afternoon he invited some fellow chief executives over to demonstrate his new on-line management information system. He gathered his colleagues around the handsome cabinet that housed the viewing screen, proudly aimed his remote control unit at the cabinet, and waited with anticipation for the cabinet doors to automatically open. After several attempts, he angrily called the Senior Vice President (SVP) of Information Systems, demanding that he send someone up immediately to get the system operating.

After several frantic and unsuccessful attempts to fix the problem, our frustrated chief executive had to embarrassingly cancel the "showing" and beg his colleagues' forgiveness for wasting their valuable time. As he packed his briefcase for the weekend, he turned to the SVP and said, "I want this fixed ASAP. I don't care what it takes!"

On Monday, when the chief executive came back to work, he was delighted to discover that his system was operating flawlessly; he called the SVP and thanked him. It was only several days later that he heard by way of the grapevine that a computer technician had missed being the best man at a friend's wedding because he had been forced to work all weekend to repair the boss's management information system. The

CEO was genuinely flabbergasted at the results of his angry demand to his SVP! Why hadn't someone told him about this? He would have been willing to delay having the repairs made.

When I was first promoted to a senior vice president's position, a wise friend said to me, "Congratulations on your promotion. However, I have some bad news and a warning for you: The bad news is that because of your lofty new position, no one will be willing to tell you the truth about anything. The warning is that people will now listen to what you have to say and they will take every word quite seriously."

We don't have to be a chairman, CEO, or senior vice president to be afforded this deferential treatment. In our work or in our lives outside of work, any time we allow ourselves to be positioned as "superiors," we are likely to set up this inauthentic dynamic.

Being a big wheel can be quite pleasurable. It's very nice to say "Jump" and have people respond "How high?" Perhaps it's annoying when people take us too seriously or overreact to our comments. But on balance the privileges that accompany being a big wheel are hard to deny. It's easy to enjoy the power and control that comes from being viewed as more important than anything or anyone else. And, if people overreact to our power and position, we can take refuge in the fact that it was not our intention to have that happen. In the worst case, we may even blame the victims by believing that it's their fault for overreacting to us.

Although being a big wheel is certainly a privilege, in fact, it is also a handicap for which we must make adjustments. By virtue of the big sword we carry, people will often be cautious, withholding, and reactionary in response to most things we do or say. If we fail to account for this reality in our interactions, there will be a price to pay in terms of lost productivity, wasted actions, and destroyed relationships.

There is a responsible way to counter the fact that people are likely to overreact to our words and deeds. Simply ask about the impact of our requests: Can this be done? Am I interfering with anything else? What is the impact of my request on you and your staff?

This takes discipline. It's not easy to hold myself responsible for asking questions for which I do not necessarily wish to know the answer. Sometimes in spite of an awareness that my requests are causing considerable stress or difficulties, I want results, so I ignore the problems that I'm causing. I rationalize that one of the perks of being a big wheel is not having to worry about these things. After all, I paid my dues and kowtowed to others for years. Now it's my turn.

As time goes on, however, I find it necessary to surrender my self-interests and self-centeredness over and over again. This is very hard for a recovering autocrat like me. It makes me feel less in control. Nevertheless, I'm becoming convinced of the negative correlation between "boss-centered" cultures and high-performance organizations. The energy spent anticipating our needs, preparing to deal with us, and reacting to our behaviors has a devastating impact on the people in our organizations.

Thankfully, I'm getting better at managing the downside of being a big wheel. I'm supported in this improvement by a growing realization that my real, long-term self-interests are best served by not behaving as though I'm the center of the universe, even if I have to "sacrifice" in the short term.

In addition to this practical and prudent motivation for change, I'm also touched by the level of intimacy and connection that comes from taking off the blinders that have shielded me from my impact on others' lives. It's very satisfying to go home at night after having made sincere efforts to account for other people's needs in my daily requests and actions. I may not feel as well served as I used to, but I feel far less lonely! I feel as though I'm becoming part of a community of people who care deeply about each other's lives.

CHAPTER EIGHTEEN

THE PROPENSITY TO BE "DEAD SERIOUS"

Business people are often very serious, very sober. We have little time for frivolity. We deal with many significant issues that weigh heavily on our minds.

We don't have to look far to justify this sober outlook on life. Our business lives are full of ominous and threatening forces like economic downturns, increased competition, demands to do more with less, and so on. These forces combined with complicated challenges in our family lives are more than enough reason to warrant our no-nonsense approach. To be anything less than dead serious, in light of these factors, could be viewed as irresponsible.

Based on our sobering discoveries about the responsibilities of adulthood, some of us warn our children to have fun now because they won't have much opportunity to be "irresponsible" when they grow up. They will have to abandon childish pastimes and deal with the world's harsh realities. In the midst of these exhortations to our children, it's difficult to determine whether we are bragging or complaining. (I think *we* sometimes forget which it is.)

Life's harsh realities do become clearer to adults. Even so, I have become curious as to why we often experience life as so heavy and harsh. What happens to the child in us? What happens to dampen our spirits? Is it possible to retain some of the optimism and joy that is more characteristic of children? Is it important to do so? Is there a place for our "child" in our adult lives?

I think it may make us feel safer as adults to focus on our problems. If we stay focused on our problems, in a sense, we have more control over our experiences because we will be able to predict and count on difficulties that we are likely to face, and we will never lack evidence that we are right. Though this may help us feel more in control, it can also cause us to spend a lot of time feeling either rageful and depressed or passive and exhausted (characteristics not widely found in children who have not had the "valuable learning" of how tough life really is).

Since we are inclined to feel responsible for virtually everything, it's hard for us to behave frivolously. How would it look for us to be having fun when there are so many serious things for us to address? There is no time when we should not be attending to business. There's always something that deserves our attention.

When we bring this very serious, sober atmosphere to our organizations, it can be quite limiting. It creates a feeling that we are hand carrying enormous loads across dangerous highways and we might get hit by a truck at any moment. Stress is up, energy is down, and risk taking can become nonexistent.

Another consequence is the impact on our creativity. At a time when we need to "play with ideas," there's not much appetite or respect for play. Such an attitude may dramatically affect our capacity for innovation.

A common technique to stimulate creativity and breakthrough thinking is brainstorming. In this methodology, people are asked to let themselves go and generate as many ideas as possible. They are encouraged to offer any idea, no matter how silly it may be. As a matter of fact, they are advised that if they don't come up with some silly ideas, the process will not likely produce breakthroughs. They are invited to have fun and enjoy themselves.

The process rarely works! Oh, long lists are generated and some good ideas do come forward. But not many breakthroughs. Most groups are painfully incapable of letting go, playing with ideas, getting silly, and having fun. If someone does come up with a "silly" idea, it is often criticized. If by chance the group does start to have fun, uneasy jokes are made about fears that someone might come through the door and catch them not being businesslike.

Laughter does not exactly ring through the halls of most organizations. On the rare occasion that laughter is heard for more than a moment, it usually attracts a lot of curiosity and uneasy attention. It is not unusual for nearby colleagues to angrily close their doors so that they can get on with serious business.

As the world shrinks and information technology floods us with data about business failures, tragedies, and unrest in all corners of the earth, the opportunities for us to become even more depressed and serious will increase. Unless we can find some way to reimagine ourselves as playful adults (currently an oxymoron), I'm afraid that the childlike spirit that guides our curiosity, inventiveness, and optimism will die—and with it, our wellness and business effectiveness.

I saw an advertisement for an amusement park that read, "A place where kids can be kids and so can parents." Could we not make this true in our companies?

We're going to have to take some fairly dramatic actions to help ourselves overcome our fixation on the difference we perceive between "adult, serious, and responsible" and "child, fun, and irresponsible." It is hard not to see them as mutually exclusive. For so many years we sat in schools and offices and obediently kept our "child" under control. But now it's possible that our wellness and our ability to creatively contribute to the world around us may be dependent on inviting our "child" back to the party.

Several years ago I hired Tony, who ran a theater program called "Acting For Nonactors," to work with some senior executives. His assignment was to loosen them up for a week of personal growth and leadership development. Tony's acting instruction was based on the premise that unless we can get people to tap into their childlike energy, they cannot unleash their capability to act with passion and creativity. He believed that *all* of life requires the same ability to access the childlike enthusiasm, risk taking, and expressiveness that acting requires.

For four hours on the first morning of our week-long leadership conference, Tony had our executives playing in an imaginary band, howling like wolves at the moon, dancing to Greek folk tunes, and creating a commercial for Harry's Hair Oil! (The latter was videotaped for the pleasure of family viewers back home.)

It's hard to convey an adequate picture of the change in countenance and spirit that these executives underwent in this short four-hour experience. Talents emerged that no one could have imagined. People who had worked together for years made connections with each other that had never existed before. The room was full of laughter and energy, energy, energy!

I remember at one point when Tony was encouraging the executives to break through their inhibitions, he yelled, "Leave the dead meat at the butcher's! Be alive...be alive...be alive!"

How can we overcome our propensity to be "dead serious"? How can we help our organizations come alive? Perhaps we'll have to begin by officially putting fun on our personal and corporate agendas. We are quite good at making things happen when we believe it's important. Let's get serious about having fun. It will be good for our colons and our competitiveness.

One executive group has a lunchtime pumpkin-cutting contest in their conference room on Halloween. The afternoon work that follows the contest has a lot more energy and spirit than on most other days.

One manager that I work with has a battery-operated "applause box" that he leaves in various offices when something noteworthy occurs. The recipient presses a button on the box and hears prerecorded cheers of appreciation. Silly? Yeah! But it brings twinkles to tired eyes.

Softball games, outward-bound adventures, after-work dance parties for staff and their partners, hiring actors to create a humorous play for the annual management meeting— if we decide it's important, we'll be unparalleled in our ability to do it.

A particularly poignant personal experience I had in relation to the importance of fun in the workplace came during very painful circumstances. I was a member of the executive committee of a major retail department store chain that had been bought out by a competitor. Every single one of the store's thirty-five hundred employees were to lose their jobs as a result of the purchase. Obviously we were faced with some very serious, very adult problems to deal with...nothing to laugh about or take lightly.

In the middle of our intense planning regarding matters like severance packages, outplacement strategies, and the like, the CEO said, "Lets have a party! Let's rent the local disco club for a night and have a party."

There was a lot of discussion about the appropriateness of a party at this time. The arguments included the fact that lots of people were mad at us for selling the business and might not feel like partying with us at this time; others said that it didn't feel businesslike under these circumstances; and some questioned the idea of wasting money on morale building when the company would no longer exist.

The CEO was persistent. He argued that these were people he cared about, we were all going through a very difficult time, and we all deserved to have some fun and relax as best we could under these conditions. "Besides," he said, "we all need each other's support during the hard times ahead."

We had the party. We discoed till dawn. We laughed. We cried. We hugged and we made promises about staying in touch in the future.

The months ahead were hard. But as we boarded up the

doors and said good-bye to the last of the staff, the party and the many other follow-up moments of support, levity, and intimacy left us all with a lightness of spirit that made the difficult times much more bearable. Actually, it wasn't just bearable, we had fun!

Coincidentally, many of us involved in the store's closing feel to this day that the work we did together during that period was one of the most effective and satisfying moments in our careers.

Adult protestations to the contrary, there is little in life that will not benefit from being perceived as a "laughing matter." As a matter of fact, fun and laughter are food for our souls and our success.

CHAPTER NINETEEN

COMPETITION VERSUS COLLABORATION

We have learned a lot about competing. We have long histories of vying for prizes such as grades, sports wins, promotions, and market share. Our drive to win is fueled on the outside by reward systems that substantially differentiate between winners and losers. Internally, we are driven by our desire to control outcomes and avoid failures.

The value of winning rarely comes under challenge. As a matter of fact, we often talk as though winning is part of a "holy war." We use language like "battle plans" to describe our approaches to overcoming our competition. It's not unusual for us to feel a sense of pleasure when a competitor fails. Whatever pain we may feel for the human beings whose lives may be severely disrupted is offset by a firm belief that there is a higher moral principle governing these situations. We subscribe to the view that we all benefit in the end if we compete freely and let the winners emerge.

These competitive battlefields are not confined to the

business down the street or across the globe. Unfortunately, the same furious competition is not unfamiliar within our organizations. As a matter of fact, the competitions are often carefully planned and orchestrated.

One large organization, in anticipation of the chairman's retirement within a year, set up an explicit competition for his position. Each of the six members of the executive office were given a chance to chair the executive committee for two months. At the end of the year, the retiring chairman would review their performance and recommend his replacement to the Board. It's important to note that each of these executives had a long history with the organization. There was little that was not known about their performance or potential.

It's hard for me to imagine what possible good could have come from this competition. The actual results in fact were disastrous. The most competent candidate for the position objected to the process and left three months into the year. People throughout the organization spent most of their energy guessing who the winner would be and making certain not to position themselves with potentially losing people or ideas. Relationships among the competing executives were irreparably damaged. The "losers" joined the ranks of "the on-the-job retired." And several years after the new chairman was named, the organization's performance sank to an all-time low. The "winner" was replaced.

Perhaps the most redeeming aspect of this situation was that it was explicit. (Foolish, but explicit!) Everyone knew the rules. Many of the competitions in our organizations are far more subtle or clandestine.

With all of the competitive encouragement and experience that we have received, we are hard-pressed to understand exactly what the growing emphasis on collaboration and teamwork really means. Collaboration, by definition, means cooperation. It's worth noting, however, the second definition of collaboration found in the dictionary: "To cooperate treasonably with an enemy."

Who's "the enemy"? Our colleagues with whom we compete for the same promotions and rewards? Other departments who may get a bigger cut of the profits if their performance is seen as better than ours?

It appears that we have a serious competitive conundrum. We have a problem for which no totally satisfactory solution exists. Even people of good intentions do not know what it means to be collaborative instead of competitive. We have built a whole culture on rugged individualism, not collectivism. Our reward and recognition systems perpetuate the problem. It's very difficult to turn off our competitive juices when we're dealing with our own organization. After all, we've been selected, trained, and rewarded for our relentless commitment to winning.

In 1986 I was introduced to an organization that challenged many of my assumptions and values regarding competition. The organization is a professional association of over one hundred consulting firms who have come together to develop and increase their capability to compete in the marketplace. These firms compete head-on in many client situations. Nevertheless, the founders formed the association on the premise that we're all better off if we're all excellent at what we do. The belief is that customers who have a positive experience with one of us are more likely to look favorably on the whole industry.

When I first started attending meetings, I fully expected to engage in "polite espionage." This was not the case. The association has created and is truly living a mission aimed at ensuring that we're all the best that we can be. Certainly, there is some withholding about things like new products we're planning to introduce to the market. However, it's a completely open book among all of us regarding how to run a successful business, how to enhance our product development process, methods for building our sales capability, and so forth. The sharing and support that I have received has been both inspiring and confusing. It has caused me to reflect on other collaborative opportunities that I and others may be missing. How has my lifelong desire to come out on top contaminated my capacity for collaboration? Am I missing opportunities to collaborate with others whom I have traditionally viewed primarily as competitors? If I wasn't always trying to win, would I lose my competitive edge?

I've begun to wonder what would change if our stated national policy was to collaborate effectively in the global marketplace. What if this policy was superordinate to "competing effectively" around the world? What would happen if we stopped behaving as though we were engaged in a war for economic dominance?

What would happen if all the automakers in the world decided to collaborate to create an extraordinarily fuel-efficient engine? Would their individual businesses suffer or gain from this action?

Such competitive conundrums present difficult decisions regarding when to compete and when to collaborate. In facing these new and unfamiliar decisions, I'm reminded of a picture that many of us saw when we were first introduced to a course in psychology: the old lady/young lady picture. When you looked at the picture one way, you saw an old lady. When you looked at the picture another way, you saw a young lady. Both ladies were always there, but it was impossible to see one while you were focusing on the other. What you were seeing at any given moment was described as the "figure." What was not being seen was called the "ground."

I'm afraid that for most of our lives we have been unable,

unwilling, or discouraged from seeing the potential for collaboration. We have been mainly focused on competing. The possibility for collaboration has always been in the picture, but it would have required us to refocus in order for it to become clear.

In increasing my capacity for collaboration, I have definitely had to become more willing to regularly alternate my focus and look for possibilities to collaborate as well as to compete. However, I believe that circumstances are now dictating an even more dramatic response. I find that for viewing the vast majority of situations that I face, I have to make collaboration the "figure" and competition the "ground."

Because life is getting so complicated, I can't really do much of anything by myself anymore. We desperately need to work together if any of us are to be successful.

Failure to collaborate for the greater good has resulted in short-term successes for many of us. Yet, we all have seen the long-term failures that have accompanied the all-out warfare, competition, and lack of cooperation that have often prevailed in so many of our endeavors. One company executive expressed his anguish over the lack of cross-departmental collaboration by saying, "I wonder how much market share we'll lose before we stop watching after our self-interests and start behaving like a team?"

I don't know how far I can or should go in my attempts to put collaboration front and center in conducting my affairs.

It feels like there are still occasions when it's fair game to "go for the kill." However, my early experiments with this new way of approaching life have led me to believe that I'm so far from recognizing and optimizing the opportunities for collaboration that it's hardly worth worrying about overdoing it!

CHAPTER TWENTY

THE PROBLEM WITH THE BOOTSTRAP THEORY

It's not difficult to believe that we have pulled ourselves up by the bootstraps. We have the desire, we work hard, we overcome many obstacles, we play by the rules, and we make it on our own. We may give some credit to our parents, a teacher, or a past boss, but we fundamentally believe that we are personally responsible for what we have become.

Though we are not ungrateful, we usually don't attribute a great deal of our success to the help we've received from others. The lifetime of support that we have received can become an invisible ally that we take for granted.

I have rarely met a person who is willing to see himself as part of the "old boys'" network. Even though many of us have the support of this network without even asking for it, there are few of us who want to admit how significantly membership has affected our accomplishments. Apparently, admission of this success factor would have an impact on our sense of self-esteem similar to that of those who are accused of getting ahead on the coattails of affirmative action.

When I was 16 years old, I wandered up and down the streets of my hometown for several days in an attempt to land my first job. Finally, I was hired to sell women's shoes in the most fashionable retail store in town. I was so proud of myself.

I went home to tell my parents about my efforts and my success in finding a job. They were delighted with the news, but in the course of the conversation they commented, "It probably didn't hurt that we knew the store owner." I felt a minor twinge of concern at the suggestion that I hadn't won the job entirely on my own. But I put these feelings aside and went about proudly broadcasting the news of my gainful employment to all my admiring friends—and as I reported on my dogged and successful job search, my parents' acquaintance with the owner wasn't part of the story. It didn't cross my mind to include this irrelevant information. As a matter of fact, over the years, as I continued to tell the story of this first job search, I conveniently left out the part of the story that might indicate that I didn't do it all on my own.

This first work experience was life changing for me. What I learned about life and business while peddling shoes on main street in Butler, Pennsylvania has carried forward to serve me time and time again, in all aspects of my life.

I don't know how significant it was that my parents knew the store owner. However, it's not hard for me to imagine that other equally capable people who didn't have this connection may have had entirely different lives because they didn't have the opportunity that I had to land a significant first job.

Over the years I have developed an image of myself that includes a compelling story of my rise from "humble beginnings." From a small town, a small college, and lower-middle-class economic roots, I can point legitimately to many accomplishments that my hard work and persistence have produced. Like many others, I have a lifetime of accumulated personal experience that confirms my belief that if you do your part, the system works. I have been largely oblivious to the extent of the invisible system of support that has surrounded me throughout all of these years. How many times did I have the advantage of this silent, invisible assistance, even when it wasn't known to me?

It's hard for those of us for whom the system has worked to relate to the discouragement and hopelessness that others may feel about their inability to get the system to work for them. To the extent that we do get a glimpse of "how it is for others," it can sometimes evoke shame or pity on our part. Neither of these emotions is very useful in helping us constructively support others to unleash their potential in our organizations.

This blindness and its implications became very clear at a conference I attended with some senior-level managers.

We had convened to discuss how to change the culture in our organizations. Key to these discussions was our widely agreed-upon need to create a more "empowered" work force. As the facilitator prodded us to explore conditions that we might need to address in our companies to achieve this desired culture change, time and again the conversation reflected the frustrated cries of the executives that the real problem was rooted in people's unwillingness to take adequate responsibility for their own actions. Any suggestion that some people might be victims of the system was not well received. Apparently, it was felt that if there is a "victim," there must be a "victimizer," and nobody was particularly willing to concede responsibility for other people's failure to make the system work for them.

Liberally spiced throughout the conversations were exhortations that employees who faced obstacles in our organizations simply needed to speak up: Stand up for yourself! Leave if you're not treated fairly. Just say no if you're being harassed. Above all, the group was resolved in its fundamental belief that if people were to behave as these managers themselves had over the years, they could overcome any obstacles and pull themselves up by their bootstraps.

Ironically, our effectiveness in creating conditions that encourage employee empowerment and self-responsibility may be negatively correlated with the degree to which we believe that we did it ourselves, made it on our own. If we cannot fully acknowledge the depth of visible and invisible support that we have, it's unlikely that we can feel much empathy for those who have not been so lucky.

Empathy versus sympathy is very important in this case. Sympathy can lead us to "parental" actions that are characterized by our doing things to and for people. Though we are willing to help, we presume that we don't need (and haven't received) much help ourselves. This maintains our one-up/one-down position of power and builds dependent relationships, rather than a good path to empowerment.

In the quality movement, there are those that believe 80 percent of human performance in organizations is determined by conditions beyond the individual performer's control. Therefore, if we want to fix performance, we should put most of our energy into fixing the supporting systems, so that individuals can be all that they can be.

As a lifelong believer in self-determination and personal responsibility, I'm constitutionally incapable of accepting the idea that 80 percent of performance may be attributable to systems issues that are beyond the control of individuals. (Maybe I can live with 45 or 50 percent.) Nevertheless, I am becoming increasingly aware of the many real obstacles that *do* exist for people to pull themselves up by their bootstraps and realize their full potential. Though many of these obstacles affect all of us, some are insurmountable for others.

Unfortunately, race, gender, sexual orientation, and religious heritage are examples of characteristics that have historically defined or significantly limited the depth of support that has been available to many people. Also, the support that wasn't available to some (because of race, gender, etc.) has been as invisible as the support that was available to others (because of race, gender, etc.).

As I have become more aware and grateful for the enormous advantages that I have had mainly due to the accident of my birth, it has *not* been necessary for me to abandon my sense of personal responsibility and pride in what I have in fact made of my opportunities. However, this acknowledgement of my advantages has made me more respectful of the problems and lack of hope that others face. And this has made it clear to me that I'm not a "better person" than those who didn't have the support that I had.

As I have abandoned these feelings that I'm a better person, I find myself more able to "partner" instead of "parent" with others who are trying to make the system work for them—because I honestly believe that the more visible support that we're collaborating to create is no more nor less than the invisible support that I have consistently received. There is no reason for anger, resentment, or disrespect for those who need help. We needed help too, and we got it!

The fact is that together we can work to eliminate

barriers, broaden opportunities, and build confidence that the system can work for everyone. And we can have confidence and faith that as we work together to clear the path to empowerment, others will be as capable and willing to pull themselves up by their bootstraps as we have been.

Acknowledgment: The thoughts expressed in this chapter represent insights that I have gained from my wife, Karen Moran, whose consulting work helps organizations create high-performance, multicultural systems.

CHAPTER TWENTY-ONE

AUTOCRATS ANONYMOUS

We are under a lot of pressure to change. People are demanding that we be less authoritarian and controlling. At the same time that we're being asked to drastically alter the management practices that we have relied on for our past successes, we're also being pressured to get more done with less resources. This is a frightening and confusing proposition.

The president of one company spoke honestly when he said, "From a values standpoint, I have no argument with the concepts of empowerment and participation. However, I'm not about to give up my controlling ways until I can be certain that the new ways of managing will produce the same or better results than my old ones. I owe it to my shareholders to be certain and I'm not convinced!"

These heartfelt remarks reminded me of the first rule of wing walking: "Don't let go of the first strut until you have your hands on the next one." Many of us don't need to be convinced that our old ways need to change, but we're not at all certain of what we're supposed to grab onto that will safely carry us into the future. And we don't know who has the answers.

Our quandary is not helped much by the fact that we don't enjoy much sympathy for the personal and professional confusion and fears we face as we try to respond to these challenges. We are the targets of considerable anger and distrust. Our attempts to change are frequently seen as inadequate or insincere. Not surprisingly, we get a little defensive and discouraged at times.

But here's a novel thought: perhaps we could benefit from creating a worldwide support group of recovering autocrats! We're not going to get a lot of help from those who view themselves as the victims of our autocratic behaviors, so why not help ourselves? Like others who form support groups, we would be more inclined to feel understood by and open to learning from those who share in and really understand our problems.

Perhaps the dream of an organization like Autocrats Anonymous is too ambitious or far-fetched. Nevertheless, it's essential that we do find better ways to encourage, support, and learn from one another. This will be difficult if we hold on to a belief that we must always do it on our own, if we view seeking help as a sign of weakness.

In my early attempts to give and get support, I took inspiration from the Twelfth Step in Alcoholics Anonymous which reads: "Having had a spiritual awakening we tried to carry the message to others and to practice these principles in all our affairs." "Carrying the message" felt less threatening to begin with because it was more akin to my old autocratic behavior. The value of getting support as well as giving it eluded me for years.

My desire to share my "awakening" led to the creation of a personal mission statement. This mission includes three words: "Witness, support, and push." To the extent that this mission statement inspires you, I encourage you to shamelessly "steal it" and put it to good use in your own twelfth-step work with other recovering autocrats.

By "witnessing," I'm speaking of our willingness to openly share personal successes and failures, emotional ups and downs, and our fears and joys, even if we're in circumstances where such self-disclosure is uncommon or risky. Silence is rarely golden and it doesn't seem to help us or others when we hide our struggles or hoard our learnings.

In "supporting," we reach out to let people know that we understand and can relate to what they are experiencing. We try to avoid conveying a phony sense of mastery or competence so that others are falsely led to believe that they are alone in their feelings of inadequacy or confusion.

Finally, in "pushing," we respectfully challenge autocratic behaviors that occur around us. This is complicated because it's not always clear whether supporting or pushing is in order. However, when we keep in mind that we're trying to help each other heal, not fix each other, we'll frequently make the right choice. And, when we're wrong, others will forgive us because they know that our hearts are in the right place.

When I first presented my mission statement to a good friend, he suggested an alteration. His recommendation was that I add "getting support" to my mission. My omission (and I might add my resistance to this addition) was a painful reminder of my long history of "preaching" rather than "reaching" for help and guidance. It's so hard and against the culture to say, "I need help." And yet, it's such a relief when we do.

I hope that we can start an epidemic of witnessing, supporting, and pushing—and, yes, getting support! An epidemic that is characterized by courageous self-examination, empathy, and support for each other; inter- and intrapersonal risk taking; and a lifelong commitment to learning and personal growth.

The principles that guide Alcoholics Anonymous are too good to be used only by those who are recovering from alcoholism: accepting how our willful controlling behaviors can make our lives unmanageable, finding a sense of a higher power to whom we can gratefully turn over our lives, taking a regular and fearless inventory of our behaviors and being willing to make amends, carrying the message to others, and practicing our new discoveries in all our affairs. And above all, knowing that we're not in this alone—if we have the courage and wisdom to reach out to people who will support and challenge us.

Recovering autocrats are engaged in a true adventure of the heart, mind, and spirit. Our journey has many of the same uncertainties that have been present for past explorers and pioneers. We're in dangerous and uncharted territory. It reminds me of the successful TV police drama that opened each show with a roll call and a review of what they were facing in the precinct that day. The final instruction from the officer of the day was, "Be careful out there. It's dangerous!" and then all the officers went off in pairs to face the day.

What a comfort to have partners whom we can count on! Let's go forward in twos, fours, eights, and tens. Call me. I'll call you. I can use the support. How about you?

INDEX

THE AUTHOR

Richard W. Hallstein spent fifteen years in retailing (Gimbels, Dayton Hudson, and J.C. Penney) and eight years in banking (Mellon Bank and Equibank), where he was a senior executive in Line Management, Human Resources, and Strategic Planning. Broad exposure to management responsibilities in these areas provides the basis for his practical solutions to challenging business issues. A further eight years of consulting to major organizations in the United States and abroad have added another valuable dimension to this experience.

Hallstein's formal training in education, organization development, and Gestalt therapy round out his perspectives on subjects associated with integrating strategic planning and human resource planning, creating participative high-performance organizations, and managing organizational and personal change.

Mr. Hallstein is CEO of McLagan International, a management consulting and training firm based in Minnesota, with offices in Connecticut, New York, Chicago, and New

Jersey. The 24-year-old company has an outstanding reputation for helping organizations develop the management processes and skills needed to transform themselves into customer-focused, quality-driven organizations.

Past and present clients in the United States include AT&T, Bellcore, Citibank, Colgate, Prudential, Schering-Plough, 3M, Time-Warner, the Internal Revenue Service, and many others. The company also has clients in Canada, Europe, and Africa.